LISTEN TO ME!

The Life and Times of a Rally Co-Driver

MIKE NICHOLSON

Published in 2013 through:

Stellar Books Publishing

www.stellarbooks.co.uk

ISBN: 978-0956508935

A copy of this book is available in the British Library

Copyright - © Mike Nicholson 2013

All rights reserved.

The moral right of the author has been asserted.

www.mikenicholson.info

No part of this publication may be reproduced, stored or transmitted in any form or by any means, electronic, mechanical, recording, or otherwise without the written permission of the author.

The views expressed in this publication are the personal recollections of the author and, in some cases, are referring to incidents which may have taken place up to 50 years ago. No offence is intended to any group or individual who may be mentioned.

ACKNOWLEDGEMENTS

My thanks to Leslie Ashe and Fergus McAnallen for their tireless efforts in sourcing and supplying many of the photographs contained in this book.

Every effort has been made to trace the origins of the photographs contained in this book. This I have managed to do in most cases with the appropriate credit given. However, there are instances where I have used personal photographs where there is no record of the photographer or copyright holder and sincerely apologise for any offence caused to the copyright holder, and will be happy to correct this omission in future editions.

Finally, I give heartfelt thanks to my wife, Marie, for all her help and encouragement and to my sister-in-law, Patricia Byron, who through her publishing company Stellar Books has been brave enough to bring it to the bookshelves.

CONTENTS

Acknowledgements	iii
Foreword	ix
The Early Years	1
The First Rallies	9
The 'Phantom Marshal'	14
The First International	17
The Yorkshire 'Mafia'	20
We Can't Let The Brits Down!	27
Give It A Blast	42
The National Caravan Rally	47
Battery Switch!	52
The Blazespeed Mini	58
If Anyone's Going To Crash....!	64
The 'All-Aggro'	69
The 'Dolly' Sprint	72
Delta Juliet Three	79
Pentti Airikkala	82
Jimmy McRae	113

At Last - A New Job!	123
He Was A Billy Coleman Fan	125
McRae Territory	134
Into The Lion's Den!	138
The Legendary Tony Pond	141
Hey, McRae, Vainqueur!	157
Wal'er Wawl!	165
What Was That All About?	175
OK Gerry, Maybe Later!	182
GM Dealer Sport	184
Terry Kaby	186
Manta Magic	200
Andrew Wood	227
Changes Afoot	238
Speed Records	241
Derek Bell - Rally Driver!	243
Listen To Me!	247
Caution, Caution, Caution!	256
1990 And Beyond	260
Make It Ice!	262
Hey You, Boy!	266
He Assumed It Was Flat!	270
Weathercock	272
Promotional Fun!	275

Triple Eight	280
Steering Is Broke!	286
Isn't It Rather Strange?	288
The Final Stage	291
Picture Credits	294
Index	297

FOREWORD

As a competitor and co-driver on UK and European rallies for 35 years, my last event being in 1992, I have been lucky enough to sit beside some of the most famous rally drivers of the time. I am occasionally asked to be guest speaker at Motor Club Dinners and Awards Nights where I recall many of the stories and anecdotes that I have gleaned during these 35 years. The audiences are, admittedly, alcoholically fuelled and easily pleased, but nevertheless seem to find them rather funny.

I have been asked many times why I have never written a book recounting these experiences. To date I have never seriously considered doing so, being of the opinion that no one would really be interested. However, now that I am retired and have more time on my hands, I have turned my mind to writing about the life and times I experienced during my rallying career.

I wish to make the point that, as some of the stories go back over 50 years, my advancing age and subsequent reduction in brain cells don't always lend themselves to recalling the finer details with great clarity especially as I, perhaps foolishly, kept no records or notes of any kind during this time.

While many of the stories are firmly imprinted on my brain, I have had to carry out some considerable additional research. So please understand this book is only intended to, hopefully, amuse and entertain the reader with some of the more interesting moments during my rallying years and should not be viewed as a chronologically accurate reference book.

I do hope you will enjoy my recollections.

Mike Nicholson

THE EARLY YEARS

I was introduced to the world at 4.00am on 22nd November 1943 at the West Hill Hospital in Dartford, Kent. At 8lb 4oz it was, by all accounts, not an express delivery! As the date suggests, Britain was heavily embroiled in World War II at the time and conditions were pretty austere. My mother was a nurse at the nearby Bexley Heath Hospital, while my father was away fighting the German Army in Belgium. He was an artillery man, towing heavy guns around the Ardennes, and generally being a nuisance to the opposition. I never found out too much about his time during the war as he rarely spoke about it. "I lost too many good mates over there," was his reasoning behind any reluctance to give detail.

However, I do remember one story when he was driving a high ranking official in a Jeep to meet with the Canadian High Command in the region.

The meeting place was to be in a forest that had supposedly been wrested from the control of the German Army. They duly arrived and, looking through the trees, saw some helmets. They were German, not Canadian! My father spun the Jeep around, shoved the senior guy onto the floor and drove flat out, weaving from side to side. They managed to escape, with bullets flying all around them, although the Jeep had a few bullet holes in it by the time they returned to friendlier territory. I believe strong words were uttered about poor intelligence when they got back behind British lines!

He was given two weeks compassionate leave following my arrival and he once said that the hardest thing he ever had to do was to return to Belgium and watch Dartford disappear as the ship left via the Thames.

Dartford was a bit too close to London for comfort and my mother used to tell tales of seeing and hearing many German bombers overhead, including the 'Doodlebug' flying bombs that rained down indiscriminately on the Greater London area.

Luckily, we all managed to survive unscathed and peace was finally declared in 1945. My father didn't return for some time, being involved in the massive clean-up operation overseas. When he finally made it back to the UK it was to find that many of the available jobs had been taken and work was hard to come by.

He eventually found employment looking after the horses at the Hinton Ampner Estate, near Alresford in Hampshire. He became a pretty good rider over the years and his employer allowed him to use the horses to compete in horse shows where he was a successful show jumper, winning various competitions throughout the south of England.

His employer's wife was also a great competitor, not only on horseback, but also in racing cars. I vaguely remember her race car – it was a highly polished, aluminium bodied Talbot and had a large aircraft style vertical fin at the back, presumably to aid straight line stability. It was a beautiful machine and it undoubtedly ignited my subsequent passion for all things connected with cars and, in particular, anything connected with speed.

My father's competitive nature was not limited to show jumping for he was also a keen driver. His employer was particularly wealthy and had one of the first Ford V8 Pilot cars to be seen on the UK roads. This was the 'E' Type of its day, with a large capacity V8 engine in the front, driving through the rear wheels. In spite of the V8's considerable displacement it produced relatively meagre power.

One winter's day, when I was about five years old, my father was despatched to the Northampton based Rice Horsebox factory to collect a brand new horse trailer and I was excited to be able to join him. It was a very cold day and, by the time we reached the high ground to the north of Newbury, it was snowing and a light build up of snow lay on the roads. Suddenly we were overtaken by a very low slung sports car (which I later learned was a French built Delage). My father was having none of that! The horns grew and we set off in pursuit, shortly catching up with the 'competition', who decided that French honour was at stake and responded at great pace. Of course, a race started, with our V8 squeezing every last bit of its power to keep up. To this day I can clearly remember standing up in the front of the car, holding onto the dashboard, shouting: "Faster, Daddy, faster!" Rest assured, I was not let down and, after a few lurid moments on the slippery road, we finally overtook the foreign invader. I was full of elation and completely in awe of my father's driving skills. I often wonder if that was the moment that sparked my longer term interest in motorsport.

By the age of six I was completely obsessed with everything to do with cars. I would wander around with my box camera taking photographs of any car that was of interest, often approaching the drivers to ask a series of mundane questions, including the obvious: "How fast will it go Mister?" I was particularly excited to capture a picture of a brand new Hillman Californian parked outside our house. It was cream, had a dark brown roof and extra large windows. The driver, a complete stranger, was parked in a lay-by, and allowed me to sit on his lap and 'steer' the car. Nothing untoward took place, of course, but how the world has changed since then! He would be feeling the long arm of the law these days!

For my eighth birthday I was given my first ever brand-new bicycle. I was extremely proud of it and kept it sparklingly clean. One day I was returning home from a friend's house when I ran wide at a tee-junction to miss a large puddle that had formed on the inside of the corner. I glanced up and the last thing I remember seeing was a black

Ford 8 right in front of me. It hit me fair and square, causing me considerable damage. I remember nothing of the impact but, evidently, I picked myself up and began to run down the road towards my home, albeit with a badly broken leg, broken arm, fractured skull, fractured cheekbone, broken jaw, crushed nose and damage to my left eye caused by bone splinters from my nose piercing my eyeball! I was bundled into the car (the poor driver was in a seriously upset state, though it was not his fault at all), and taken to the local GP. He realised the seriousness of my injuries and immediately called for an ambulance which rushed me to Southampton General Hospital. A local market gardener was despatched to find my father who was exercising a couple of horses and was found two miles away. The poor animals were tied to a fence and left to their own devices while my father rushed home, collected my mother and drove flat out to the hospital. Bones were set, many stitches placed in deep cuts on my face, and operations carried out to save the sight of my left eye.

I had the best part of two years off school and had a couple of other corrective operations during that time but, eventually, I fully recovered. You can imagine how it later coloured my mother's view of anything to do with my involvement in motorsport!

Shortly afterwards my father was offered a job in Derbyshire and we moved to a small village, Sudbury, some fifteen miles west of Derby. I attended Sudbury Primary School where the headmaster, 'Gaffer' Hallam, seemed to take a dislike to most of his pupils, including me. He was a true tyrant and ruled with a well aimed bean-bag and liberal use of the cane.

I later attended the brand-new John Port Grammar School in Etwall, near Derby. The new students, including myself, arrived on day one feeling rather nervous. It was completely daunting, especially as the teachers wore caps and gowns which made them look extremely fierce, as indeed many of them turned out to be. It was a good school however, and I enjoyed the social side of grammar school education, especially with one rather lovely pupil named Fiona. We 'met' when our unruly classmates locked us both in a broom cupboard where we spent a good couple of hours in close company (if you get my drift) before we were let out. I was never a great academic at school and had no interest whatsoever in the mundane subjects we were forced to study. Geography and Physics were my favourites, but I pretty much 'bombed' at everything else!

It was during this period that my motorsport 'career' began, mainly with the intention of attracting girls. Sadly this objective turned out to be singularly unsuccessful!

THE FIRST RALLIES

At the age of 14 I met Stan Ratcliffe, the 'petrol-head' son of a local farmer. He owned an old Ford Thames van and, like me, was a big motorsport enthusiast. The van had a side-valve 903cc engine, delivering very little power through a three-speed gearbox, with a huge gap between second and third (top) gear and it was slow in the extreme. Nevertheless, Stan had learned the knack of driving it pretty quickly and we had many wild journeys back from the local youth club, racing with other similarly clapped-out vehicles. Basically, he never lifted his foot off the throttle, and we nearly always won!

We decided it was high time we joined a motor club and entered a few competitions to prove our mettle. We duly became members of the Brailsford & District Motor Club, based near Ashbourne in Derbyshire. This was quite an active club, with a disparate group of enthusiasts taking part in all manner of competitions, including sprints, autotests and, of course, with the fabulous roads of the Peak District on the door step, road rallies.

I remember our first attempt at rallying. It was a wet, misty and foggy night-time road event starting from the Club's home village of Brailsford. Now, those who remember these old Ford vans will know they had vacuum powered windscreen wipers, fed from the inlet manifold. However, there was a problem with this system. If you drove flat out, which after all is a requirement for competitive activities, the wipers would stop! Lift off the throttle, and they would go ten to the dozen. There was, therefore, a skill involved in balancing the two ends of the spectrum with careful use of the throttle in order to balance the maximum performance with the maximum visibility.

Sadly, Stan had yet to master this particular skill and one mile from the start, in heavy rain and little visibility, flat out with the wipers in the stopped position, we failed to see a right-hand bend and went off the road, demolishing the gatepost at a farm entrance. The van rolled onto its roof. We scrambled out and ran to a safe distance, expecting it to explode in a fireball at any moment, in true movie style. Then we heard screams of "STAAAN!!!" coming from inside the wrecked vehicle – we had completely forgotten Stan's long suffering girlfriend Josie who had been in the back sitting on the old mattress that, for some reason, Stan kept there. We dragged her out and were confronted by a very angry farmer. Any hopes of a sympathetic hearing were dashed when he chased us down the road with a shovel!

This, and several other mishaps with rather incompetent drivers, including another 'off' with Stan's brother in an Austin A40, made me realise that, if I was going to be killed, I would rather it was me at the wheel at the time.

By now I was living in Uttoxeter and had joined Unigate as a salesman, working from their large depot based in the town. There were four of us and we each had our own geographical territories to work in. The role involved selling dairy produce direct from a van to grocery shops and small supermarkets. My 'patch' was Staffordshire, Shropshire and the Potteries. It was a most enjoyable job - the only downside was putting up with the rather slow Morris Commercial 3 Ton van that was my mobile sales office. I would load the van every morning with boxes of butter, cheese, cream and other dairy products and set off to sell my wares.

Luckily, the old Morris Commercials were soon pensioned off and replaced with a fleet of brand new 5 Ton Bedford TK vans. Although these were a huge improvement, they were governed to a maximum of 55mph, which to a budding rally driver was rather frustrating.

The depot had a large workshop where the fleet of delivery trucks and vans were maintained, and I went out of my way to befriend a couple of the mechanics. I needed more speed, and I managed to persuade these lads to modify the engine's governor. They worked miracles and, thanks to their efforts, I drove the fastest TK in the country, easily capable of 65mph!

As soon as I had scraped enough money together I bought a rather ancient Ford Anglia 105E, one of those with the peculiar raked-back rear window. It was a completely standard car and the only modification I could afford was a sump guard. Nevertheless, I finally had my own rally car and was reasonably quick and, with my navigator

Mick Price, won several night-time road rallies. Unfortunately, simply being quick was not enough, and the ability to temper my speed with any modicum of sense was completely absent. Several costly mistakes were made – too often (to quote a well used phrase) my speed overtook my talent halfway round a bend! My two mechanic friends at the depot were also enthusiasts and worked wonders to keep the ageing and abused Anglia going. Eventually, my main sponsor, my local Lloyds Bank Manager, decided I had one too many red figures on my statements (come to think of it, they were all red!) and pulled the plug on my rallying career. I eventually sold the car for £90 to my future brother-in-law, whereupon it promptly fell to pieces two weeks later. We didn't speak much after that.

So, it was back to the navigator's role and I spent a few more years competing in road events, up to and including the Motoring News Championship rallies, with a variety of drivers, again of differing ability.

THE 'PHANTOM MARSHAL'

Mike Broad (who went on to become a highly successful co-driver) was a member of the Shenstone Car Club and we joined forces to organise the Shenstone Rally, which had become part of the prestigious Motoring News Road Rally Championship. We spent weeks in the hills and dales of Derbyshire sorting out a fantastic 200 mile route for the overnight event, finding several new 'white' (unclassified) roads to test the crews.

In the early hours of one morning, while checking the route on a remote 'white' road, we stumbled upon five or six travellers' caravans blocking our way. We hastily turned around but found our route blocked by several men armed with sticks and pitchforks! We had to be pretty quick with our explanation for being there – they were not the friendliest bunch of people, but eventually they let us pass! The Derbyshire Peak

District had become a very popular area for night-time road events and we had to avoid several PR 'black-spots' following complaints from local residents. One chap found a unique way to make his protest and disrupt events. He became known as the 'Phantom Marshal' and we were rather nervous that he would make an appearance on our rally.

His method was simple. He would find out when a rally was to take place, discover the route and drive along part of it until he found a time control. He would chat to the marshal to gather all the details he needed and then back-track half a mile to set up his own, unofficial, time control. He had all the right gear including official looking control boards and his own sealed watch. The competitors would pull up, assuming the control was a little 'off plot' and receive a time. Roaring into the night they would pass the official time control a little way down the road, refusing to stop and commenting: "Oh look, there's the Phantom Marshal!" In the meantime the poor marshal at the official control was tearing his hair out as the cars swept past! After a dozen or so cars had gone through, the 'Phantom' would disappear, having successfully screwed up the results! This went on for the best part of six months and no-one ever discovered who he was. One day he just disappeared and was never seen again. Brilliant!

Luckily, he avoided our rally, which we were pleased to find was a great success.

THE FIRST INTERNATIONAL

In 1968 I joined the renowned South Derbyshire Motor Club and met Mike Osborne, whose father was a wealthy soft-drinks magnate from Burton-on-Trent. Mike was keen to take up special stage rallying in his Cortina GT and we competed on several events in the Midlands area, including the famous Dukeries Rally. The Cortina was a bit long in the tooth, so Mike bought the wreck of a Mk 2 Lotus Cortina which had been written off in an accident. A new Mk 2 body-shell was purchased and we spent the whole of the winter in his driveway, working under a large tarpaulin, rebuilding the car into the new shell. It was cold work and, on one particularly freezing evening, we emerged at midnight to find we were buried under six inches of snow! The car was eventually finished and we set off on a new episode in our rallying careers by entering the dizzy heights of an international rally.

Our first international was the 1970 Welsh Rally, for which I had to upgrade to an International Competition Licence. At the time I had a company owned Ford Cortina 1600, so I borrowed the sump guard from Mike's rally version and, bolting it to my unsuspecting employer's car, competed on the requisite number of events! Luckily, the car remained unscathed, though I remember panicking when a photograph of the car, complete with rally plates and numbers on the doors, appeared in a Motoring News report of an event that we won in East Anglia. Luckily no-one of note saw it!

The Welsh brought home to us just how hard international events were on both the car and the crew. It gave us little respite over its three days and two nights, and tiredness became so all-consuming that we occasionally hallucinated! One night we turned into a forest road, leading to the start of a stage. Mike stopped and began to reverse out.

"Where are you going?" I asked.

"I can't go down there," said Mike, "there's a Pickford's removal van in the way!"

There was actually nothing in the road at all, but he had definitely 'seen' it! Other than that, the event was singularly lacking in any memorable incidents, and we managed to finish a fine forty-sixth overall.

THE YORKSHIRE 'MAFIA'

A major change took place in 1970 when a new sales job, with Imperial Foods, took me to live in Boston Spa, Yorkshire. We moved to a brand new house, beautifully built with stone from a demolished Huddersfield cotton mill. We had some great neighbours, with one or two practical jokers among them. The house had a long drive, so we bought some tiny apple trees, about three feet tall, and lined the driveway with them. A couple of weeks later we returned home to find all the trees laden with apples! Puzzled, I looked closer and discovered that various neighbours had each bought a pound of apples and tied them to the young trees with fishing line! On another occasion, we returned home and my three-year old daughter said: "Look, there's a bird on our roof." Sure enough, there was! It was a huge stuffed stork, tied to our chimney, which had been placed there by our next door neighbour, who happened to be a merchandiser for a package holiday company. Amazingly, it was only three weeks later that my wife announced she was pregnant again! They are truly fabulous people in that part of the country.

I had no regular rally driver at that time so I joined the Yorkshire 'Mafia' – the Rallying 'Mafia' that is. I was freelancing and sat beside various leading Yorkshire rally drivers, including David 'Piggy' Thompson, Colin 'Mad Dan' Grewer, Tony Drummond, Peter 'Yuk' Hodgson and the terrifying Dennis Pelling. These drivers were all very talented but had no high ambitions beyond having a ball on every rally they took part in! Piggy Thompson and Tony Drummond, in particular, stick in my mind and my liver still protests to this day.

I was co-driver for Piggy (he was a successful pig farmer) on several stage events. One, the Border Rally, started and finished in Hawick, with stages in Kielder Forest. For the life of me, I cannot remember where, or even if, we finished the event – it's all alcoholically blocked from my memory. I do remember the journey home though, with the Escort on a trailer towed by Piggy's Volvo

Estate. We were all terribly hung over and Yuk Hodgson, who had been servicing for us, pleaded to stop to relieve himself. For the fun of it Piggy refused. Eventually Yuk was so desperate he threatened to empty his bladder inside the car, so we found a lay-by on the Northumberland moors near Otterburn. Yuk leapt out but, while he was mid-stream, David floored it and, with wheels spinning, we set off with Yuk running after us, still in a state of undress. He leapt onto the back of the trailer, determined not to be left behind – if he hadn't done so there's little doubt he would have been left there, such was the 'humour' of the Yorkshire 'Mafia'. I can still hear the string of abuse coming from the rear of the trailer as Yuk clung on for dear life at over 60mph. We eventually persuaded Piggy to stop half a mile later and let him back in the car. How he didn't die that day, no one really knows! They were all completely bonkers!

Accidents will always be a part of rallying and we had a particularly scary one on another event in Kielder Forest. The car spun, rolled and ended upside down in a deep culvert at the side of the forest road. Our problem was compounded by the car becoming jammed against the sides of the culvert, preventing the doors from opening. There was a junction off to the left, just at the point where we had rolled. The front windscreen was hard against the 'wall' of the secondary road, with the car at an angle that prevented any exit through either the front or rear screens! There was no way out of the car and we were trapped, which was pretty scary. I switched off all the electrics as there was a strong smell of fuel and, tempting though it was to blow the horn to attract attention, we didn't want to risk any spark setting off a fire. That would, undoubtedly, have been the end of us.

It was frightening stuff and several cars passed at speed without stopping, though in fairness they probably couldn't see our car. Luckily for us, the system for counting cars in and out of the stage worked and after quizzing several other competitors about our failure to appear at the end of the stage and, with nobody having seen us, the Stage Commander sent in a rescue van. Thankfully, they found us and manhandled the car enough to enable an exit through the rear screen. The feeling of claustrophobia from having no escape route lived with me for some time.

There would often be riotous after-rally parties in our hotels. We stayed at one particular hotel in Newcastle upon Tyne after taking part in the Lindisfarne Rally where the hotel bar was modelled on Lord Nelson's cabin on his famous ship, the Victory. At the entrance to the bar stood two dummy cannon – not the real thing but, nevertheless, exceptionally heavy. It was felt these would look better on the hotel roof, so a group of us reconvened in the early hours, after the bar had shut. The hotel was built on a split level, with one part being four storeys high, the other, six. The two cannon were placed in the lift and taken up to the fourth floor, where one of our team had a bedroom. They were then manoeuvred out of the bedroom window and onto the flat roof. Ropes were brought from a service van, while several others found the stairs to the roof of the taller half of the hotel. Both cannon were then hauled up to the second level, and then even higher still, to be finally placed on top of a large water tank.

The next morning, all hell let loose! Police were called and several people quizzed. We all protested our innocence, but one hotel porter, a pleasant little chap, was convinced of my involvement. In a very broad Geordie accent, he kept pointing at me: "I know you were f**kin' involved, I just f**kin' know it!" he ranted. "If it wasn't so f**kin' serious, it would be f**kin' funny!"

We got away as soon as we could with no charges being laid against us!

We had a bit of bother on the Granite City Rally too. We were staying at the Tall Trees Hotel in Aberdeen. The hotel had a small lake just outside the main entrance. The management had placed some plastic decoy ducks on the lake in the hope that the real thing would be attracted and bring some wildlife to the hotel gardens. It never seemed to work, until this one particular year. We arrived to find that no less than six live ducks had made a permanent home there. The hotel management were very pleased with their success.

At around two o'clock in the morning, after the event, a Scottish rally driver, Hamilton 'Hammie' Hannah, a rather wild man straight out of the Highlands (who was renowned for cutting down more trees than Basildon Bond) dived into the lake, grabbed a couple of the ducks, and marched into the bar, dripping wet, with one duck under each arm. The birds were rather distressed by all this activity so Hammie let them go in the reception area. They flew out of the door into the dark and snowy night, never to be seen again. The next morning, the only ducks to be seen on the lake were the decoys. There was a lot of trouble about that!

Another highly rated Scottish driver, Drew Gallagher, was known to be a bit aggressive after drinking alcohol and would often start a fight in the hotel bar. Once everyone else in the bar was involved, he would quietly slip out of the fracas and leave the rest to it until the police arrived! Sadly, Drew is no longer around, but he was a great character, and a good chap to have on your side if there was any trouble!

WE CAN'T LET THE BRITS DOWN!

During 1971 I met Roger Platt, a very quick driver from Redditch. He rallied a 1760cc pushrod single-cam Escort at a considerable pace and was notching up some success in stage rallying. I asked if he knew of anyone looking for a co-driver for the forthcoming Welsh International Rally – he told me that, actually, he was, and invited me to do it with him. Roger had a considerable reputation and I was not sure that I was experienced enough to sit alongside him. He insisted it would be fine, so I gratefully agreed. The event went well and we finished a strong seventh overall behind the winner, Tony Fall, and other luminaries such as Will Sparrow, Colin Malkin and Tony Fowkes.

Roger was also taking part in some Motoring News road rallies and had entered the Red Dragon Rally, which started in Tredegar. I was asked to navigate for him, following my experience of reading Ordnance Survey maps in Derbyshire road rallies in previous years. As we approached the small Welsh town we had an altercation with another driver who cut us up in a rather aggressive manner. A short-tempered exchange followed and we told him where to go in no uncertain terms. He drove off rather chastened and left us both feeling pretty pleased with ourselves.

We arrived at scrutineering to find that the Chief Scrutineer was.......well, I don't have to spell it out, do I? Suffice it to say that he found at least six faults on the car, including a leak from the fuel tank. It was obvious he was not going to let us start so we threw in the towel and returned home.

Nevertheless, flushed with our recent success on the Welsh International, Roger and I, along with Russell Brookes and co-driver Kevin Gormley, entered the Sherry Rally. This was a punishing event, starting from Jerez de la Frontera in Southern Spain, using stages in and around the Sierra Nevada range of mountains. This was a big step up for us, never having tackled a foreign event before – and what an eventful rally it turned out to be!

Roger had to find a new tow-car to pull the trailer the 1400 miles from Redditch to Jerez, via the Portsmouth to Cherbourg Ferry. Roger's trade was used-car sales, and he quickly found an old Vauxhall Victor Estate. This was the first model of the Victor, with the wrap around front windscreen. These early cars were built using a dodgy batch of Japanese steel and became rather renowned for excessive corrosion (Vauxhall soon dropped their "Salute the Victor" advertising strap-line!). Nevertheless, it looked smart enough from the outside and the car seemed to fit the bill perfectly. I think Roger paid £12/10 for it!

The big day came and, with near enough two tons of rally car and spares on an un-braked four-wheel trailer, with the Victor packed full of four adults and much more in the way of servicing equipment, we set off. The first part of the journey was pretty straightforward, with a nice smooth ferry crossing to boot. We disembarked in Cherbourg and set out on the longest leg of the journey, some 1200 miles to Jerez. On the road out of Cherbourg there was a slight incline, with traffic lights at a crossroads, which were on red. Roger was driving and we pulled up and waited for the lights to change. Pulling away, with a lot of revs required for the rather high first gear of the three speed gearbox, there was a strong burning smell from the complaining clutch. As the car edged forward there was also a tremendous 'bang' and the whole car seemed to stretch an extra foot. All the doors burst open and one of our two mechanics, who was dozing, very nearly fell out onto the road. I was sitting in the rear and lifted the carpet to see what was going on. I was somewhat concerned to see that the floor had split from one side to the other and there was a large gap through which I could see the road.

Undaunted by this development, we continued, with a couple of bungee straps holding the doors closed. However, it was not lost on us that the car was only being held together by the roof panel which, by now, had a considerable crease across its width. Nevertheless, the roof seemed to be holding at this point, so we proceeded, rather unsure of whether we would actually be able to reach the next town, let alone Southern Spain.

As we were discussing our situation, a lady in a Citroen 2CV pulled out of a side turn, right in front of us, causing Roger to stand on the brakes. The car slowed a little and then two tons of trailer and rally car caught up with it. There was another loud 'bang' and the offside front suspension collapsed.

We pulled to the side of the road to inspect the damage. Having jacked up the car we could see that the badly corroded front wishbone suspension arms had given up the ghost under the additional stress. They had pulled out of their mounts, leaving their fixing bolts in-situ, allowing the whole lot to collapse. This was serious, because we had only completed six miles from the ferry and still had a very long way to go. Not to be beaten, however, we set about knocking the whole lot back into place.

We, rather irresponsibly, cut some pieces of wire off an adjacent fence, wrapping them round and round the 'repaired' wishbones. We tack welded the repair and set off rather gingerly. Amazingly, the car held together and the only other problems we encountered during this mammoth journey was that the heater control became stuck in the 'hot' position with outside temperatures close on 30 degrees, and then becoming hopelessly lost in Seville. Having taken a wrong turn, we found ourselves in a mass of one-way streets, each one narrower than the last. Eventually, with panic rising and with the trailer wheels straddling both pavements and pedestrians having to squeeze into doorways to let us pass, we found our way back to the main road! We arrived at our destination, Jerez de la Frontera, after three days of rather intense driving!

We found our cheap and rather down-market motel, which had little to offer other than a massive swimming pool, and where the staff turned out to be both rude and arrogant. We were rather inexperienced overseas travellers, so we tended to take their attitude on the chin. The biggest offender was the so-called head waiter, dressed rather pompously in a somewhat scruffy uniform. He was surly, extremely aggressive towards us and proceeded to give us a hard time, ignoring our many requests for service when we wanted a beer. Revenge would be sweet......!

Roger and I set out the next morning to hire a car for the recce. We had allowed ourselves two weeks to cover the considerable distance of the rally and, as we had little money, settled for an old Fiat 600. This small and rather underpowered car, which could barely stagger up some of the higher passes in the Sierra Nevada, nevertheless tackled the job with gusto and took all the punishment meted out with total reliability. The air conditioning consisted of a canvas roof that fully rolled back.

The stages varied in surface and condition. Some were pretty smooth running through miles of olive groves on sandy roads, some ran over very high mountain roads (up to 9000 feet) and some were on very rough and little used cart tracks. They were spread across an area to the north of the Costa del Sol, with the route running through some very isolated parts of Southern Spain. On one occasion we were running very short of fuel and, it seemed, miles from civilisation. We eventually came across a tiny village and asked a group of locals where we could buy some 'gasoline'. They pointed to a small shop across the road and, sure enough, the proprietor allowed us to buy a few gallons from churns that he kept in a shed!

We were fascinated to see houses built into caves, with mud walls, and with blankets hanging across the doorways to keep the elements out. One night, after we had been driving for miles and miles with no sign of life whatsoever, we crested the brow of a hill to see a small village ahead. It was brightly lit by the presence of a huge funfair, with thousands of people enjoying themselves and most having presumably journeyed from many miles away. It was a very strange sight in the middle of such remoteness.

Eventually, the recce was completed so we returned to Jerez and back to our hotel. The Escort had been lovingly attended to by our service crew during our time away and actually looked rather resplendent in its garish green paintwork. Unfortunately, the application of rally plates and various rally sponsors' decals did little to hide the fact that our rally car was beginning to look a little the worse for wear after a hard life. Nevertheless, it was quick and reliable and we were pretty confident of a good result.

Scrutineering was completed with no problem but, overnight, some of the locals decided to strip all the decals from the car and we had to hurriedly find replacements the next morning.

The start ramp was situated in front of the local Sherry Board's Headquarters, on a rather splendid palm tree-lined avenue. There were thousands of spectators lining this 'avenida', several deep for as far as we could see. We were seeded Number 6 and as we waited in line, car Number 1, a seriously expensive and very quick Porsche 911, belonging to a local millionaire sherry exporter, Antonio Ruiz Jimenez, drove down the ramp. It stopped. Then, with the engine on the rev limiter, the clutch was dropped and two black lines were left on the road, accompanied by a great deal of tyre smoke, as the car shot off into the distance at high speed. This was merely the start of the first road section and not a special stage! It was too much for the thousands of locals, who went crazy with excitement and demanded the same from the next group of starters, including ourselves.

"We can't let the Brits down, can we?" said Roger, as we slowly drove down the ramp. On reaching the tarmac, Roger floored the throttle, dropped the clutch and the car lurched forward, accompanied by the demanded wheelspin and much tyre smoke............and, alas, with a dreadful and terminal sounding 'rattle' from the engine! Something was seriously wrong! We slowed and crawled down the boulevard, listening to jeers from the disappointed locals, and to dreadful noises coming from the car. Once out of sight of the hoards of local enthusiasts we stopped and lifted the bonnet. There was oil everywhere. The engine, which had been newly rebuilt for the event, had thrown a con-rod. We were out of the rally, just one mile from the start ramp!

We were devastated. All those miles travelled, all the mishaps suffered in discomfort on the drive down to Southern Spain, sweating in the super-heated old Victor and after all the time spent on the recce, we had managed just one mile of road section! Hugely disappointed, we retrieved the trailer, loaded up the Escort and retired to the hotel.

We changed out of our overalls and met by the pool for a much needed beer (or six!). Sure enough, our arrogant waiter friend was even worse than usual. He had little respect for us before but now, after such an obviously dismal effort on the event, we were not worthy of any attention whatsoever. Ignoring us several times as he passed by, we finally snapped, leapt up and, with one hand on his collar and one on his trousers, heaved him into the pool, complete with his tray.

Feeling somewhat satisfied by our revenge, we began to feel even better as we watched the waiter thrashing around in the water, the frustration built up during the morning's disastrous events, gradually diminishing.

Something was odd, however, and our attention was drawn back to our 'friend' in the water. We were amazed to see how fast he could swim. He raced up the very large pool using a rather strange butterfly style stroke, with his back arching up and down like a giant dolphin and weaving from side to side. Mark Spitz would have had some considerable difficulty keeping up with him as he powered along, almost up on the plane. We watched in awe and the first inkling we got that all was not well was when he head-butted the far end of the pool and sank in a load of bubbles!

Shocked, we ran around, jumped in and pulled him out.......only to find he was in the middle of an epileptic fit! Not our finest hour I'm afraid. Luckily for us there were no witnesses to point the finger and he seemed to remember nothing of the incident. I'm pleased to say he made a full recovery. We were pretty chastened and kept a low profile after that. We certainly never asked him for another beer!

Eventually the Rally finished and the competitors returned to Jerez. Russell Brookes did well in his Mini, finishing fourth overall. The lavish prize-giving ceremony was being held in the Sherry Board's amazing headquarters and we all set off in the Fiat 600. I say all, because we gave a lift to some of the other competitors staying in our hotel. There were nine of us in total, five inside the diminutive car and four sitting around the opened sunroof, enjoying the cooling breeze, with just their legs dangling inside! This did little for the car's suspension, already weakened by the two week recce. It squatted down on its haunches, with the dipped headlights dazzling everyone coming towards us. Unfortunately, this included a member of the Guardia Civil, who promptly turned around, gave chase and stopped us. Our driver was arrested and taken to the local 'cop shop' where he was relieved of several thousand pesetas by way of a fine and a reprimand. This left us with very little money for the return journey.

The prize giving ceremony was a grand affair, full of local dignitaries, as continental events usually are. There were a few speeches, none of which made any sense to us, being conducted in Spanish. The guest stars of the show, one of Spain's top flamenco dance groups, were introduced onto the stage to much applause from the appreciative Spanish audience. They were very good but, by now, we were all pretty high on the free sherry, generously donated by the event's main sponsor.

Russell decided that, while they were good, he could do better and promptly joined them on stage, performing a very comical version of the great Spanish dance. The group was not at all amused and, to huge cheers from the audience, Russell was dragged off the stage by some burly officials. I do seem to remember a scuffle followed as some of us thought Russell had been handled rather roughly, but that's all a bit vague now! At least there were no more arrests.

We set off the next morning and luckily had a much less eventful journey home. We were, by now, completely spent up with just enough money for fuel and none left for decent meals. Once back in Redditch the old Victor was welded up, and even sold at a profit – typical Roger!

In November we took part in the Lombard RAC Rally, starting in the Yorkshire town of Harrogate. We were again using Roger's green Escort, with the engine rebuilt (yet again!) following its Sherry Rally failure. We completed the first day's spectator stages with no problems. Roger was on form and, with the Escort proving to be reliable, we were running just inside the top twenty. As the rally moved north it started to snow and, by the time we arrived at Stang Forest in the North Yorkshire hills, it was lying very deep indeed. We set off on the stage and, about half way through, the car ran wide on a fast left-hand bend, digging into the soft snow, which dragged us into the ditch. Roger kept his foot in and steered hard left in an effort to regain the road. The car hit something in the ditch, leapt out, and before he had chance to straighten up, it shot across the road, down a steep bank and hit a tree. The tree shuddered with the impact and deposited a ton of snow onto the car! We were completely stuck, out of the event and even had difficulty opening the doors having been buried in snow!

Several hours later, the Stage Commander and his Rally Rescue crew pulled us back onto the road. The car was still driveable, so we met our service crew at the stage finish. It was now two o'clock in the morning and we set off in the vain hope of finding accommodation in Consett. We came across the Railway Hotel, a rather run-down looking place, which was in complete darkness. We rang the doorbell several times, more in hope than anticipation. Eventually, a light was switched on and the door was cautiously opened by two ladies. We explained our situation and they let us in. They were fantastic and cooked us a full English breakfast before once again retiring to bed. They even opened the bar and left us an 'honesty pad' on which any drinks we had were detailed. We retired to bed and discovered that the bedrooms were unheated and absolutely freezing. We slept in our overalls and anoraks!

GIVE IT A BLAST

I continued to co-drive for various members of the Yorkshire 'Mafia' during the early '70s. I joined Colin 'Mad Dan' Grewer to compete in the Dukeries Rally in his famous Volvo Amazon. Colin was a very quick driver and we were lying inside the top five when, half way through the Clipstone Forest's longest stage, the throttle linkage fell apart, leaving the throttle stuck wide open. Having only just survived the ensuing 'moment', no doubt still imprinted in the memories of a dozen or so spectators who thought their time on earth was ended, we drove the rest of the stage using the ignition key as a throttle. We either had full throttle or nothing but, somehow, Colin managed to complete the final two stages in this manner, using the starter-motor to get the car off the line, with the Volvo's engine backfiring furiously in protest every time the ignition was turned off and on!

The York National was one of the better stage rallies, aided by the close proximity of the fabulous Yorkshire forests. The 1972 event was particularly memorable! I was co-driving for Piggy Thompson, who had sold his Escort and replaced it with a Porsche 911. The car was rally-prepared but had a pretty standard engine, with standard gearbox and final drive ratios. This gave it a very high top speed. The rally was based in Scarborough, only thirty miles from our home town of York, so after scrutineering, which was completed successfully, we drove home. We noticed that the engine had developed a high-end misfire and, once we got onto the A64, Piggy decided to 'give it a blast' to see if it would clear. We shot past a police car sitting in a lay-by at around 130mph! Of course, it took off after us with blue lights flashing.

We stopped and two policemen approached. They were pretty angry but calmed down a little as Piggy explained about the misfire and promised he would be more sensible in future (yeah, right!). The book was out and they prepared to issue a pretty damning ticket. They were, however, rather interested in the rally and began asking questions about the event - what were the stages like, what speeds did we achieve in the forests and so on? I had an idea:

"What are you doing tomorrow?" I asked.

"We're off duty and thinking about spectating on the rally," one said.

"OK, here's a plan. Why don't we meet just before the Harwood Dale stage and we'll do a swap. One of you can sit in the co-driver's seat and do the stage in the Porsche, and the other can drive me to the end of the stage, where we can swap back again."

Piggy looked on in amazement but, incredibly, they agreed and the ticket for speeding was cancelled! This was highly irregular and heaven knows what possessed me to suggest it. Thankfully, they too had second thoughts and were not at the pre-planned rendezvous point the next morning. There was relief all round!

Yuk Hodgson had entered the same event in his Mini Cooper but, a couple of days before the start, the engine dropped a valve, which did untold damage. Not to be thwarted, Yuk found a second-hand standard 850cc Mini engine from somewhere and replaced the wrecked unit. The 'Cooper' was now very slow but Yuk tackled the event with typical gusto, working up a lot of sweat for very little reward!

The York National usually held one stage on the Oliver's Mount motorcycle race track on the outskirts of Scarborough. It is a fine tarmac stage, running up the side of an escarpment. It's very fast and undulating along the bottom section, followed by a couple of uphill hairpins, leading to a very long straight across the top. It then runs back to the start area via a further couple of tight downhill hairpins. The event demanded just two laps, before peeling off at the end of the long top straight to the finish. It might not sound like much of a stage to the purist but it was actually great fun and did have the potential for producing a very nasty accident! We roared off from the start, with Piggy really going for it. Thundering along the top straight on lap one, with the Porsche pulling well over 100mph, we came across Yuk in the painfully slow Mini. He spotted us in his mirrors and began weaving from side to side to prevent us passing! We were having none of it and forced him onto the grass, overtaking him with a series of rude gestures.

Yuk, however, was enjoying himself so much that he decided to carry on for another lap.....then another....and then another! The Stage Commander was going ballistic, waving all sorts of flags at him and trying anything to get him to stop. After ten laps they gave up and just left him to it. I don't know how many laps he finally completed before calling it a day but we never saw him again during the rest of the event. He's probably still up there now!

THE NATIONAL CARAVAN RALLY

It was around this time that I tried something very different. I was asked by a York motorsport and caravanning enthusiast if I would navigate for him on the forthcoming National Caravan Rally in his Volvo, towing his Sprite caravan. If you think that this particular caravan rally consisted of a group of mobile home enthusiasts camping in a field, please think again! This was indeed something entirely different - basically, it was a 'blast' around England and Wales at high speed with a 'box-on-wheels' in tow! I believe there were only three such events before they were banned, two starting from Silverstone and the third from Mallory Park Race Circuit in Leicestershire. It was this latter event that we entered.

In the 1970s caravans were pretty Spartan boxes but, nevertheless, any unnecessary equipment was taken out, and the competitors ran as light as possible. There were, however, strict rules concerning eligibility. They had to have a gas supply, a working oven and a fully operational toilet among other 'essential' items. One keen competitor saved additional weight by removing the chemical loo completely, replacing it with a shovel in the toilet compartment. It was deemed by the scrutineers to be legal, evidently!

We couldn't modify or damage the Sprite though, as it was in regular use for family holidays. There were factory entered teams and I particularly remember the works Bessacarr Caravan team even had fully equipped service vehicles chasing their entries around the route.

Leaving the Mallory Park start, the event ran on a variety of roads across the Midlands, before crossing the border into North Wales. Crews had to maintain a strict timetable and there could be no dawdling if the tight schedule was to be adhered to. In fact we were pretty well flat-out everywhere. The route became decidedly more difficult in Wales, with outfits having to squeeze through many miles of narrow Welsh lanes. Many of the roads were bumpy, with tight corners, hairpins and steep hills.

To be honest, you didn't really need a navigator for this part of the event - the drivers simply had to follow the trail of wreckage! We were seeded midfield and running about fortieth on the road. The carnage had to be seen to be believed! There were gas bottles and jockey wheels littering the lanes, towing mirrors and various bits of caravan and car bodywork too. Fibreglass 'wool' insulation was seen hanging from roadside bushes, after caravan side walls had been ripped off. On one tricky downhill section, which ended in a tight right-hand bend, there was a complete caravan axle, with wheels and leaf springs still attached, lying in the ditch halfway round the corner. A few hundred yards later, the remains of the caravan was parked off to the side of the road, lying on its 'belly'! The tow car was still attached, with the stranded crew waving forlornly at the passing competitors.

We managed to avoid any real problems and finally arrived back at Mallory Park, worn out, after a solid 48 hours on the road. Then followed the 'piece de resistance', a caravan race! Sadly, navigators were not allowed in the cars for this, so we all gathered trackside to see the fun. And fun it was! Most of the caravans were fitted with a stabiliser called The Mongoose (kills snakes – get it?) and the trick for the race was to tighten it down to its maximum, thus preventing any movement in the hitch and basically creating a single six-wheeled vehicle! There was still some skill required by the driver, however, who needed to keep an eye in the mirrors for any sign of the caravan's inside wheel lifting in the corners, and easing off on the steering wheel to prevent disaster. There were some drivers who had not fully developed this particular skill, and yet more caravans were destroyed by the inevitable roll!

After the race was finished surviving crews had an hour or so to prepare their caravans for the Concours d'Elegance. The manufacturer's support crews went into overdrive and many caravans were presented in 'as new' condition, having been comprehensively rebuilt in the paddock! Our Sprite was a bit long in the tooth and wasn't the smartest around, so we didn't bother to enter against such immaculate competition.

It was an amazing event, which to my knowledge, was never held again, following many complaints of caravans being driven at high speed across the country's highways and byways. It's a real shame because it was great fun!

BATTERY SWITCH!

I sat alongside the legendary, York based, Tony Drummond on various national forest events. Tony had just one stage start procedure. As he used to put it: "I rev it to eight thousand, drop t'clutch, and dig two bloody great 'oles in t'road!"

He was a very talented driver, though he did seem to have a slightly cautious approach to the ultra-quick stuff. This was fine on the twisty stages, but it did lose him some time on the long straights.

One of these events was the Lindisfarne Rally, a classic national stage event held in Kielder Forest. The Escort's BDA engine was not the newest around and, in spite of Tony's protestations that it was using a lot of oil because: "I like to build 'em loose," in all honestly, I think it was pretty tired.

The crankcase compression, perhaps due to worn piston-rings, was such that the two gallons of oil in the dry sump tank were being totally lost through the crankcase breather in a dozen or so stage miles. We faced a further problem, which I pointed out to Tony in one service area: the next stage, Wauchope, was 18 miles long and we would run out of oil half way through! Drummond being an ingenious engineer came up with a plan. He fixed a long pipe onto the breather, securing it with a jubilee clip. He then bent the nearside rear corner of the bonnet upwards and routed the pipe through the gap and into my partly open window. The other end of the pipe went into an empty one-gallon oil can, which was to be held between my legs! The plan was to stop mid-stage when the can was full, empty the contents back into the oil-tank, and then complete the final six miles or so. A novel plan indeed, and, in spite of my reservations, we set off for the stage.

I mentioned earlier that Tony could be a little cautious on the ultra-quick stuff and was, occasionally, reluctant to select fifth gear, so I'd given him a bit of a talking to at the service area. We were lying fourth but going backwards due to the very high-speed nature of the Kielder stages. In a determined mood, we set off into the forest, adopting one of the usual 8000rpm starts and initially everything was fine. The oil was being recycled nicely into the empty Castrol can held between my legs but it was rapidly filling up, becoming very hot and causing me some serious discomfort. Around the three-quarters full mark it became very painful to hold on to the can. My problems were compounded as it reached these upper levels when, every time the throttle was floored, the compressed air from the crankcase blew through the pipe, along with the oil. This caused the contents of the can to bubble like a witch's cauldron and the interior of the car (and me) was being covered with very hot lubricant.

In the midst of all this I was trying to read the stage off the oil soaked map (no pace notes allowed in those days) while being scalded by the red-hot oil in the can. Nevertheless, I was just about managing and, from the map, I could see that we were about to embark on a very long straight section of the stage.

"C'mon Tony, fifth - take fifth, it's straight for nearly a mile!" I urged.

With a loud grunt he slammed it into fifth gear and floored it. We absolutely flew down the straight, flat out, with hot oil spraying all over the interior of the car!

The road went over a brow and down into a dip – it was a real roller-coaster ride! In the bottom of the hollow, unseen by either of us, was a large bump on the right-hand side of the road. With the front suspension on compression there was no travel left and, at well over 100mph, the car hit the bump and simply took off. It climbed high into the air and gradually pitched forward, crashing to earth on its roof and punching the roll cage through the floor of the car. A series of barrel rolls followed, end over end, side over side, with the accident seeming to go on for minutes. The rear axle left the car, followed by the engine and gearbox. We rolled over some rocks which punched their way through the roof, creating some very sharp 'spears' of metal sticking down into the car. Eventually, we hit some trees and stopped, all quiet except for the whirring of the fuel pump.

"Battery switch!" wheezed Drummond, in pain with broken ribs.

"BATTERY SWITCH!"

His voice was now rising in panic amidst a very strong smell of fuel.

"I can't see it, where is it?" I desperately enquired.

"It's behind you." he wheezed.

Idiot, I thought, it's below the dashboard, how can it be behind me?

"IT'S BEHIND YOU!" roared the wounded Drummond, just like a pantomime audience.

It was then that I realised my seat had broken away, turned around, and I was facing backwards! Then my own panic set in - I was covered in something hot and sticky! I was so convinced it was blood and I was mortally injured that I daren't look down. Eventually it dawned on me that it was the red-hot contents of the full can of oil, which I had let go of during the accident, that had emptied all over me! It was a big relief!

It was a huge accident - the biggest in my 35 years of rallying. I had four or five baths when we returned to the hotel but I still couldn't remove the impregnated oil from my skin! It was such a legendary shunt that Autosport Magazine dedicated a whole page to it, complete with pictures.

I absolutely loved my ten years living in Yorkshire and accompanying these fabulous guys on the various rallies. I recently saw some current

Historic Rally footage on television and it's good to note that some of these 'Mafia' originals are still going strong. Bob Bean, Steve Bannister, Peter Smith and Chris Birkbeck are still at it and still crashing their cars at pretty regular intervals!

They may be considerably greyer these days but their advancing years has, in no measure, diminished their speed.

I was recently treated to a shake-down in Peter Smith's fabulous Mk1 Escort. This was the first time I had sat in a rally car, being driven in anger, for fifteen years and I was shocked at the power, traction and handling of the latest evolution of this classic rally car. Peter assured me that we were going to have a steady run but if that was a steady run then I wouldn't want to be sitting in the car when he was trying! I'm much too old now to take such punishment over any distance but Peter's driving was most impressive. It's easy to see why Historic Rallying has become so popular with spectators over recent years.

THE BLAZESPEED MINI

I joined Russell Brookes for the 1972 Welsh International Rally in his Mini Cooper S. Russell had a pretty feisty relationship with his regular co-driver, John Brown, and they would often fall out. One such falling out occurred just before the Welsh, so I was asked to shoehorn my six-foot plus frame into the diminutive car. Russell was a very quick driver, especially in a Mini, and we were going well.

However, leaving one service area to tackle the tarmac Epynt stages, having had racing tyres fitted, we found the car was handling badly. On right-hand bends the oversteer was appalling. We stopped to investigate and were not amused to find that the mechanics had fitted three slick racing tyres, but had forgotten the near-side rear wheel, which was still fitted with a worn forest tyre! We turned around and flew back to the service area where the embarrassed lads fitted the correct rubber!

Once back in the forests, and during a particularly wet and foggy night on the Crychan Forest stage, we failed to spot a downhill tightening right-hand bend in the poor visibility. We rolled over the edge and down into some trees, ending our rally on the spot. It was a shame, because sitting beside Russell had been very entertaining.

It was through Russell that I met Pat Ryan. Pat hailed from Jersey, where his family owned several hotels and the British Leyland franchise in St. Helier. At the time he was rallying a 1300cc Morris Marina. Its diminutive 100bhp engine was married to a four-speed gearbox and had a Jim Whitehouse designed eight-port cylinder head. Fuel was fed to the engine by the rather unusual set up of four Amal motorcycle carburettors! In its class it was actually quite a good rally car and I joined Pat to co-drive on a few national events. Being rear-wheel drive the Marina handled quite well, with just enough power to promote oversteer and for us to pretend we were actually in a works Escort!

We tackled the 1973 RAC Rally, but all was not well with the engine - it would only run on three of its four cylinders. British Leyland had supported us with the loan of a works service crew for the event and the mechanics changed everything but it became obvious that the problem was not electrical. Suspicion eventually fell on the Amal carburettors which, for some reason, flatly refused to submit to the mechanics efforts to balance them and we completed a large part of the event on three cylinders! After that experience, the car was changed to a more conventional set-up.

Pat then commissioned, what was to become, the ultimate Mini of its time, the infamous Blazespeed Mini. Blazespeed was a rally-preparation company run by Roger Smith, an ingenious engineer, based in Birmingham. They were tasked to come up with an ultra-competitive rally car, based on the Mini Cooper S. They more than achieved this and, to be honest, it was lethal! It bore a strong resemblance to a rally-cross version. It had no front or rear bulkhead, a hardboard dash to keep the elements out and the roll cage holding the car together. The dashboard had a habit of popping out mid-stage allowing any lying water to spray inside the car covering everything; maps, timecards and the crew, in large quantities of mud!

The full Mini rear beam was removed and replaced with a small alloy crossbeam, with two trailing arms hanging from it, and motorcycle style spring/shock absorbers providing the rear suspension. The roof was made of fibreglass to save yet more weight.

The engine had offset bores, allowing the capacity to be taken out to some 1340cc without compromising the integrity of the cylinder block, and an eight-port head fed by twin Weber carburettors. The whole car weighed around 13cwt and, with an unheard of (for a Mini) 100bhp at the wheels, the power to weight ratio was amazing.

While it was a pretty dangerous car to take into the forests (or indeed anywhere there was something to hit!) it was massively fast and quickly gained a reputation among spectators as being the one to see! Pat was an awesome driver, hanging on for dear life to this beast of a car, which spent much of its time trying to kill us! It was, however, ultra-competitive.

We took it to Scotland to compete in the Granite City Rally, an event based in the forests around Aberdeen. We'd had a great rally and we were leading overall, ahead of Roger Clark's Escort, with just two miles of the last stage, Durris Forest, to complete. Then disaster struck! Pat left the braking too late for a tight 90 left bend. We hit a bank head on with the massive impact ending our rally on the spot. Pat confessed afterwards that he was 'miles away' at the time and dreaming of collecting the trophy for the car's first win! A tough lesson was learned. Shortly afterwards we did rather better on the Castrol Timpson Rally and brought the car home to its first win, in front of John Price's Renault Alpine.

There were some lighter moments though. On a Welsh rally we were dawdling through a small village on a road section between two stages. We noticed an old chap, probably in his seventies, standing by the side of the road, dressed in a beige smock and leaning on a hoe. We smiled and waved at him. He seemed to take offence at this and rushed forward, slamming the hoe down onto the roof of the Mini! The hoe punched a hole through the fibreglass and embedded itself firmly in the roof. The old boy was determined not to lose his implement and hung on tightly as he was dragged down the road at 20mph. Eventually, he let go and, unharmed, dragged himself to his feet, screaming obscenities at us in Welsh! We didn't dare stop because a lynch mob was gathering so we continued for a few hundred yards until it was safe to do so, where I promptly removed the offending implement and placed it on the side of the road. The old chap was determined to 'have' us and was running down the road as fast as his old legs would take him, still shouting obscenities. We hastily left the scene, still not knowing what his problem was!

IF ANYONE'S GOING TO CRASH...!

During 1974 I continued to rally with Pat but was asked by the one-time Polish Champion, Marek Gerowski, if I would co-drive for him on the Welsh International Rally, an event that was not on Pat's itinerary. Gerowski had purchased an ex-Bjorn Waldegard works Porsche 911.

I'd had little experience of a Porsche, apart from the earlier York National with Piggy Thompson, so I was pleased to take up the opportunity. We were allowed pace notes for the Epynt Ranges that year (I think! We made them anyway!). Marek had a rather unique pace note style. Instead of describing the road he would note which gear to be in for any particular corner, and then allocate a speed to the note - for example, 'fast, very fast or flat' etc. A sequence of his notes would read something like:.......right 3 (gear) very fast, 100 left 4 medium into left 2 slow, 300 right 5 flat into left 4 medium........and so on. A different style, yes, but it actually worked pretty well.

Early in the event we drifted wide on a particularly narrow bend in Radnor Forest and brushed against some foliage on the right-hand side of the road. The car stopped dead, all electrics lost. We fiddled with everything we could think of but to no avail. Then I spotted that the exterior electrical shut-off switch was in the 'off' position. The branches that we'd brushed against had knocked the switch off, killing all the electrics stone dead! The car immediately fired up when it was switched on again and we were away, unfortunately having lost many minutes in the process. The car and crew remained reliable after that and we eventually finished tenth overall.

The Welsh Rally, at the time, was particularly tough, consisting of three days and two nights of non-stop action throughout the entire country. Sleep was almost impossible to come by, apart from a couple of snatched hours at the, so called, 'rest halt' in Machynlleth during the second night. A few miles into the final road section on the M4, and heading to the Barry finish, we were in such a state of fatigue it physically hurt. The car suddenly veered off the motorway onto the hard shoulder. Gerowski's adrenaline level had, by now, dropped and he'd fallen asleep!

"C'mon, get out," I insisted, "I'll drive."

We swapped over. Less than five miles later the car veered off onto the hard shoulder again, as I, too, was overcome by tiredness and nodded off.

"Get out," insisted my weary driver, "if anyone's going to crash this car, I will!"

The Welsh Rally was held during late Spring, my favourite time of year, when the trees are many different shades of green. However, it remains the only home international that I didn't win, even after some sixteen attempts. I was second or third a few times but the win always eluded me. It was a fabulous rally though.

The 1974 RAC Rally was tackled with Piggy Thompson now back in a Ford Escort which had been added to his collection of rally cars. On the third stage, the Harewood Hill Climb, all drive failed, as the half-shaft departed from the rear axle. It disappeared, complete with wheel still attached, over a hedge and down a hill! A Motoring News photographer captured the moment when the half-shaft departed and the picture took a prominent place in their write-up of the event.

As you can imagine, we were a bit miffed at having retired so early on, but it had its compensations. We later turned up as spectators on a stage being held in a park just outside Bradford, where the Mayor had erected a large marquee for council guests. We managed to infiltrate the hospitality unit and became quite merry drinking vast quantities of tax-payer funded champagne, which somewhat helped to numb the disappointment!

It was around this time that Piggy's long-suffering wife, Barbara, gave birth to a son, James. I was not to know it at the time but, many years later, in my capacity as Vauxhall's Motorsport Manager, I employed James to drive in our BTCC Team. 'Thommo' became a very successful racing driver and won the British Touring Car Championship twice, both times driving one of our Astra Coupe race cars. David, his father, was justifiably proud of his son.

I joined Tony Drummond for the 1975 Welsh International Rally in his Escort RS. It was good to be back with the Yorkshireman again. Budgets were tight, however, and we completed the whole event on Motorway Remould forest tyres. These tyres were actually not too bad for forest use but left a lot to be desired on the thirty or so tarmac miles of the Epynt Range stages! The rear tyres wore down to the canvas in a very short time and this resulted in some extreme sideways driving. With most of the other competitors running on racing tyres, we were certainly more entertaining for the spectators! Nevertheless, we were pretty pleased with our twelfth overall.

THE 'ALL-AGGRO'

In 1975 Pat Ryan received a phone call from John Davenport, the Motorsport Director for British Leyland, who had noticed his results in the Mini. Pat was invited for an interview at BL's Abingdon based motorsport headquarters where he was offered a role as a team driver, with me as his co-driver. It was our first 'works' contract and we were over the moon, not only looking forward to driving a Dolomite Sprint but to being paid as well! There was a twist though. We were told we would not be driving the 'Dolly' Sprint but would spearhead a new project to develop a brand-new rally car. This sounded pretty exciting and we eagerly awaited details. John Davenport (known as JD within the team) eventually unveiled the new car. We were shocked – in front of us, in all its glory, was.......an Austin Allegro!!

Once the initial shock had worn off, and we

looked closer, it was actually not a bad car. The Cooper S had been all-conquering in its day and this Allegro 'variant' had all the main components from the classic Mini.

The car actually turned out to be pretty quick. Its long wheelbase, with wheels at its four extremities, ensured good handling and, with a Cooper S engine installed, it went pretty well too. It was, however, rather heavy and this turned out to be its Achilles heel. During testing the additional weight proved too much for the transmission. First, the drive shafts failed, so they were strengthened. Then these new shafts passed the additional strain further into the transmission and various differential components failed, time after time.

Several National Championship forest rallies were attempted, unsuccessfully, the transmission failing on every event. In spite of this we were entered on the 1975 RAC Rally, with the car having had its drive-line further beefed up. Sadly, it was to no avail, and we only lasted a few stages before all drive was lost on the Oliver's Mount stage near Scarborough.

The team persisted with the car into 1976 and we took part in the Snowman Rally based in Inverness. Here, once again, the 'All-Aggro' transmission failed and we were stranded in Rosedale Forest, near Elgin. Brian Culcheth and Johnson Syer, our team-mates, were still running strongly, and our service crew was pulled away to give them extra support. It was decided that our car would be picked up later and we were instructed to find our own way back to Inverness! When we asked JD how we were going to get there, he shrugged his shoulders and told us to use our initiative, so we hitched a lift to Elgin station with some spectators. We sat on the train for Inverness, looking embarrassingly conspicuous in our rather muddy overalls, crash helmets in hand and with other passengers looking on curiously.

We attempted one final event but, unfortunately, the same fate befell the car. We had failed to finish a single event with the Allegro due to its transmission problems and it was finally decided to scrap the programme.

THE 'DOLLY' SPRINT

At last we got our hands on the Triumph Dolomite Sprint, in time for the 1976 British Open Championship season.

The car was a Group N variant of the Dolomite, with the associated technical limitations of the class rather pegging the car's performance. The biggest problem was the brakes, which consisted of discs on the front and drums on the rear. The braking performance was not too bad in the forests where the retardation stresses were not so severe but on tarmac it was a different story. After about six miles on any tarmac stage the rear drum brakes would overheat and 'fade out' completely, transferring the full braking load to the front discs. These would then follow suit and disappear within a further few miles due to overheating. On the longer stages it was a nightmare, there being virtually no stopping power after ten miles or so. It was very frustrating, but within the Group N technical regulations we were not allowed rear discs, nor were we allowed an adjustable brake-balance system to assist with braking distribution. Nevertheless, we found an ingenious way around the problem........I could tell you how, but then I'd have to kill you!

Our first event in the Dolomite was the Mintex Rally, which started from Harrogate and it went wrong from the start! The first stage was in the Harrogate Show Ground and, around half a mile from the end, the engine stopped! The fuel pump had packed up! We were determined not to give up and set about pushing the car to the stage finish. Luckily there were thousands of spectators and many took it in turns to help push the car to the end. We had lost a lot of time which unfortunately compromised the rest of the rally for us, but at least we were in a Dolomite!

In June, we flew north for the Scottish Rally, which included a rather odd stage known as Glen Kinglas. It was a dead straight broken tarmac road of approximately two miles in length, which ran parallel to the main highway. It did, however, contain many, many jumps and some were pretty severe. We pressed the car over these crests as quickly as we dare, but one caught us out. It was colossal! The car leapt high in the air and crashed down nose-first into the unyielding tarmac. All seemed well until we arrived at the service area immediately afterwards, where we found that we were unable to get out of the car! The shell had bent and all four doors were jammed tight, after which we had to enter and exit via the windows. JD was not best pleased as the car had to be re-shelled after the event!

1976 had seen the introduction of the Triumph TR7 into the British Leyland Team. Tony Pond, with Fred Gallagher co-driving, was brought in to drive one car, with Brian Culcheth and his long term pace note partner, Johnson Syer, in the other.

'Culch' used to tell the 'story' of how he met Johnson Syer. Evidently, he was out in his car one day, ran off the road and crashed into a distillery. When he drove out the other side, he found Johnson sitting beside him in the passenger seat!

Johnson was a great guy and we enjoyed some very interesting nights with him! I remember sharing a room with him in the Aviemore Post House Hotel during a Scottish Rally. I woke at

7.00am to find him fully clothed and standing by the door.

"Where are you going?" I asked.

"Going?" he said, "I'm just coming in!"

Later, I was told he had been seen in the 'wee small hours' sliding down the artificial ski slope on a hotel tray, singing at the top of his voice! He looked terrible but a couple of hours later he was alongside Culcheth and setting off for another day in the forests – some stamina!

The TR7 was an awesome looking car, with the early models powered by the Dolomite Sprint 4 cylinder, 16 valve engine. The car was rather difficult to drive, with its very large shallow and sloping windscreen, giving the crew the impression that they were sitting in the back seat. Visibility was further compromised by sitting so low in the car. The handling of these early cars was not great and it was generally a bit of a disappointment. As a result, Pond and 'Culch' struggled to achieve decent results during the year. It never really hit the 'sweet spot' until the mighty V8 was launched the following year.

It was decided to enter Tony and the TR7 in the September York National Rally to test some modifications prior to the forthcoming RAC Rally. Fred Gallagher was not available to do the event so I was very pleased to accompany Tony and have my first experience of both the car and driver. The rally started in front of the beautiful Castle Howard stately home (well-known for being the venue for the TV series 'Brideshead Revisited' some time later) and ran in the classic North Yorkshire forest stages. However, the first stage began just 100 yards from the start ramp and ran through the extensive grounds of the estate.

We very nearly came to grief on a fast tarmac section across open ground, within a mile of starting this first stage. Flat out over a crest, which hid a tricky left and right chicane, we straight-lined the corners, got well out of shape and very nearly ended our rally there and then! We just got away with it thanks to Tony's legendary skill behind the wheel and survived to fight a mighty battle with Tony Drummond in his Escort RS through the ensuing forests. It has to be said, Drummond just had the edge and, although there was little between us, it seemed we were destined to finish second.

Then we saw his Escort parked up at the side of the long Dalby Forest stage, with 'Drumbo' making extremely rude gestures as we passed. It seems he had cut a corner and ploughed through a very large pool of standing water, which had drowned the engine. He was instantly out of the rally. "I could have drunk that puddle dry through a straw," he complained, when we caught up with him later. It was, however, the first ever win for the TR7 and everyone (including JD) was pleased with the result. I thoroughly enjoyed co-driving for Tony and we got on well, our sense of humour gelling nicely.

I took a short break from my British Leyland duties, with John Davenport's permission, to compete on the 1976 Dukeries Rally with Piggy Thompson in his Porsche 911. It was a beast of a car and very quick down the long straights of Clipstone Forest on its standard gearing - I swear the speedometer read 140mph at one point! We enjoyed a fabulous run and brought the 911 home for an outright win. Piggy was a very talented driver but, sadly, never took rallying too seriously, being too intent on enjoying the high life that came with it. I believe he could have gone on to a works drive if he had put his mind to it.

Sadly, David Thompson and Colin Grewer are no longer with us, but no doubt they are still going flat out on that great stage in the sky and causing general mayhem! Their heavenly Stage Commander will be tearing his hair out trying to control them!

Come November, it was time for the 1976 RAC Rally. Pat and I were in the Dolomite as usual and, by mid-event, we were lying a strong ninth overall, pulverising the Group N opposition. The team was looking forward to a top ten finish. We were leading the Group N class by a mile, and perhaps should have approached a ford in one of the Kielder Forest stages more cautiously - it was obviously very deep.

Several other competitors had 'drowned out', the crews milling around with very wet feet, trying to restart their engines. We decided to 'go for it' at speed - it was a mistake! Water was sucked into the engine via the carburettor inlets and it 'hydraulicked', bending all the con-rods and ending our rally there and then! The service lads in the team were distraught and, as you can imagine, once again JD was not best pleased, especially as the engine had just been rebuilt for the event!

DELTA JULIET THREE

Pat and I continued to use the Dolomite Sprint on the 1977 British Open Rally Championship. We had some reasonable results, including ninth overall on the Welsh International Rally and several class wins. In the lead up to the RAC Rally Pat had spent a considerable amount of time bending John Davenport's ear, trying to persuade him to prepare a third TR7 for us to use on the forthcoming event. Constant dripping finally wore away the stone and we were presented with a pristine TR7 for the UK's premier rally, which started for the first time from Wembley Stadium. However, it was not to be a happy event for us.

There was a lot of pressure on Pat to put in a good showing. Unfortunately, this led to several minor 'offs', losing us considerable time. This was uncharacteristic of Pat, who was normally pretty safe, and the more JD growled at us, the more mistakes were made. Tony Pond began to 'take the piss', and at a service area somewhere in Wales, the radio crackled into life:

"Delta Juliet three (us), this is Delta Juliet one (Pond), do you copy?"

"Affirm," I replied.

"Are you on your own?" he enquired.

"Yep." I replied. There was a pause...........

"How many times did you go off on that one then?" he said roaring with laughter!

He could be a cruel so and so and was delighting in our misery.

Shortly afterwards we were waiting in line at the start of the Clocaenog Forest stage in North Wales. A delayed Timo Makinen was starting the stage behind us and strode up to Pat's open window.

"Ven I catch you, you vill move over!" demanded the Finn.

"Who does he think he is?" retorted my stressed driver, after Makinen had gone back to his Fiat 131. "He's got to bloody well catch us first!"

Unfortunately, it didn't take long! We spun on a tight corner and lost a fair bit of time turning round. All too soon Makinen's lights were behind us and the aggressive Finn was 'pushing' us to get out of his way. After a mile or so of increasingly wild driving I persuaded Pat to let him pass and we stayed wide on a narrow left-hand junction. I put my hand out of the window to wave him by. Makinen hesitated, not sure whether we really meant it. Pat took his hesitation as an invitation to continue and floored it, just as Makinen did the same! He drew alongside and there was a collision. Unfortunately, my arm was trapped between the two cars and I suffered some really painful bruising as a result. Rallying is such fun!

We were finally put out of our misery when the gearbox seized on the M6 near Carlisle. It was a merciful release and ended our last event with the British Leyland Team.

PENTTI AIRIKKALA

Shortly after the Manx Rally during September, John Davenport had taken me to one side and had told me, confidentially, that our contract would not be renewed for the following year. I was, of course, very disappointed but was somewhat cheered when he said he would recommend me for another seat in a works car if one came up. I was sworn to secrecy and was told, categorically, that if I ever breathed a word of it to anybody, he would see to it that my works rally career would end there and then! I believed him and kept the secret for several weeks until the announcement was made.

JD was a hard man on his drivers but generally had a good relationship with the co-drivers. He had been a world class co-driver himself and had empathy with them. I don't know whether he had any input behind the scenes but, soon after the RAC Rally, I returned home to be told Gerry

Johnstone had phoned and would I call him back.

Gerry was the competitions boss at Blydenstein Racing, the company that was to run the Vauxhall Chevettes, under the Dealer Team Vauxhall banner, in the 1978 British Rally Championship. The name 'Dealer Team Vauxhall' came about because the necessary budget was raised by way of a levy placed on the dealer's invoice for every new car that was sold. The levy only amounted to a few pounds for every vehicle and, to be honest, the budget was always tight.

Gerry was a rather quiet individual and an excellent engineer but was well-known for being rather difficult to converse with during a telephone conversation. There were often long gaps in any dialogue. I called him:

"Hi Gerry, it's Mike Nicholson."........long pause!
"Hello Gerry, are you there?"
"Yes Mike.".......long pause!
"Hello Gerry, can you hear me?".......long pause!
"Yes Mike."................long pause!
"Gerry, you asked me to call you?"...long pause!
"Yes Mike.".........long pause!
"Well, I'm calling you Gerry!"
"Yes?".................long pause!

"Oh yes......would you like to co-drive for our Finnish driver this year?"

"Who do you mean?" I asked.

"Pentti Airikkala, of course!"

He didn't have to ask twice even though it took him ten minutes to get to the point! I was over the moon and it was agreed that I would go to the Blydenstein workshops in Shepreth for a meeting with both himself and Pentti. I must confess that, while excited, I was also somewhat overawed by the prospect of sitting beside such a rallying superstar. I arrived at Shepreth a few days later and the contract was agreed, initially for one event, the Mintex Rally in February. If all went well I would also be doing the rest of the season with him, with the exception of the Manx Rally, where English pace notes would be a problem.

Our team-mates in the second Chevette were to be Jimmy McRae and co-driver Ian Muir.

The 1978 Mintex Rally was a very memorable one for me. It's always a daunting prospect changing to a new team, with new management, new mechanics and a completely new environment. On this occasion, there was the additional pressure of joining a new driver too. Not just any driver but one of the legendary 'Flying-Finns', and one who had a reputation for being a bit fiery! In fairness, Pentti went out of his way to make me feel welcome. I was invited to stay overnight at his rather splendid house in Cookham Dean, Berkshire. His wife served up a magnificent meal before retiring to leave the men to talk!

"Vould you like a drink?" enquired Pentti.

"Yes thanks, a whisky and dry ginger would be great."

He returned shortly afterwards with a tall tumbler filled to within an inch of the top – I could already feel a headache coming on but I took it and raised a glass to our new season.

"Vait, vait, vait," said Pentti, "you need some dry ginger in there!"

The next morning I felt dreadful, completely wasted. Had I been stopped by the police on the way home I would, without doubt, have been arrested for a drink-driving offence.

February soon arrived and we made our way to the Harrogate start of our first event together. In the late '70s the British Rally Championship entry list consisted of the cream of rally drivers and included many of the World Championship contenders:

Markku Alen in the Fiat 131, Hannu Mikkola, Roger Clark and Ari Vatanen in Escorts and, of course, the usual crop of British drivers, Pond, McRae and Brookes among others.

I constantly reminded myself that I was very much on trial during this event and was determined to make a good 'fist' of it. I had made considerable efforts to get myself in shape, physically and mentally, and it seemed to pay off. Having a very good knowledge of the Yorkshire forest stages I was able to read them off the OS map, almost as accurately as having full pace notes. This was a new experience for Pentti. He was impressed that I knew all the 'flat' crests, blind corners and firebreaks that were waiting to catch out the unwary. At the halfway halt in Scarborough I insisted on staying with the car to oversee the work to be done, while Pentti snatched a couple of hours sleep in a hotel which, again, seemed to impress him. Dedication to duty and all that!

We had a good battle with Mikkola who, while it was close, generally had the upper hand. However, he suffered some mechanical problems, which left us arriving at the last stage - a two mile thrash through the tracks of Rudding Park on the outskirts of Harrogate - with a good overall lead.

"Pentti," I said on the start line, "we have a two minute lead, with just the two miles of this stage to complete, so I hope you will take it easy."

"Of course," he replied, "I vill drive like Grandma, but I have to say to you, vatever happens, you are the best co-driver I have ever had!" I was full of pride!

We set off, but he drove like a crazy man, absolutely on the ragged edge, much to the appreciation of the thousands of spectators and much to my concern. Mid-stage, he cut a corner and hit a bump on the inside at considerable speed. The car lifted way up onto two wheels and we very nearly rolled within sight of the finish. We completed the stage in tears of laughter and with some considerable relief! It was a great win and I soaked up the glory of our achievement, with Pentti's positive endorsement of my co-driving ability still ringing in my ears. I had passed my 'trial' with flying colours, and my contract was extended to the end of the year.

Our next event was the Circuit of Ireland Rally, held over Easter. In those days the Circuit was a monster of an event - there were 55 stages, totalling over 600 stage miles, held over five days throughout the whole of Ireland. It was really tough on both car and crew. It was during this event that I was to witness the other side of Pentti's temperament. He arrived in Belfast in what can only be described as a dark mood. For whatever reason, the 'Mintex Pentti' was nowhere to be seen. He was angry about everything and barking orders at everyone within earshot which, unfortunately, on many occasions included me!

The rally was not good for us, or indeed for some of the other luminaries on the event. Brookes went off on the first stage, losing five minutes and Mikkola later retired with broken transmission. We had an axle leaking oil onto the rear brakes for the first few stages and Pentti's mood darkened even further as we lost considerable time. It was being made worse by the fact that Jimmy McRae, our team-mate, was beating us hands down.

Everyone in the team was walking on egg shells and keeping their heads down, trying to avoid Pentti's attention. He called me every name in the book! I was useless evidently and everything that was going wrong with the car was my fault! I was a bit distressed about this, because, in my view, I was doing exactly the same job as I had done on the Mintex. I was rather taken aback by this previously unseen side (by me, anyway!) of my new driver.

Things did improve over the next couple of days though and gradually his mood lightened. He was driving well and we were gaining some of the earlier lost time and lying inside the top five, but with Jimmy still leading the field.

One particular stage stands out for me. Known as Arigna Mountains, it is one of Ireland's classics. On this occasion it was over thirty miles long and tackled at night-time. It was raining hard, with visibility particularly poor over the mountain top, where thick fog had formed. Pace notes were not allowed and the Irish maps had little or no detail worth trying to read. It sticks in my mind to this day, that over those thirty miles, in truly appalling conditions, four drivers (Airikkala, Alen, Mikkola and Brookes) driving different types of cars and, with no pace notes, all recorded a stage time within four seconds of each other. Incredible!

Irish spectators always turned out in their tens of thousands for the Circuit. Unfortunately, they didn't always think things through terribly well!

On one stage, the only road to the start was completely blocked with cars. It appears that hundreds of spectators had arrived at the stage and parked down one side of the approach road. Others then arrived and parked down the other side. Eventually, late-comers drove all the way to the stage start, between the two rows of parked cars, found there was nowhere to park and left their cars in the middle of the road, completely blocking it! The rally cars had no way of reaching the stage and the co-drivers had to run well over a mile to receive an arrival time. Of course, the stage was cancelled, so it was the enthusiasts that lost out in the end. Manic!

We arrived at the Killarney rest-halt feeling a bit better with ourselves. Pentti was trying to be apologetic to team members and invited me to go for a sauna with him. This turned out to be a big mistake - never have a sauna with a Finn! It was bloody hot! Walking down the hotel corridor, looking for the sauna, Pentti stopped a porter, resplendent in his green jacket and asked:

"Excuse, please, is this real Finnish sauna?"

"Ah sure," the little guy replied "the whole hotel's been finished for four years now."

Pentti just stared at him!

The rally restarted but, unfortunately, another thirty mile night stage saw our downfall. The stage started in a valley, climbed fifteen miles up one side of a mountain and over the top, before running the last fifteen miles down the other side. Pentti was, by now, fully back on form and we were absolutely flying. However, after a few miles, he said over the intercom:

"Mike, get torch!"

"Now, shine on my feet and look at this!" he said still going flat out.

I watched as he pressed the brake pedal......it went right to the floor! There was no retardation whatsoever. Under the circumstances, I suggested he might like to slow down.

"It's OK, it's all uphill," he replied.

"Yes, Pentti, but in four miles it all goes downhill," I quipped.

"Ah! You vorry too much!" he retorted.

Inevitably, it was only a matter of time, at this unreduced pace, before we would go off the road, and I had plenty of warning of the approaching accident! The section of the stage was straight, dropping steeply downhill for several hundred yards and leading to a tight 90 right bend, which was easily spotted in the lights. Without brakes there was absolutely no possibility of us making the corner and we went straight on, punching through a hedge, with the nose of the Chevette dropping vertically into a small river, some two feet deep. We hung there in our seat-belts for a few seconds surveying our situation and it became obvious that there was no way for us to continue, we were too far off the road.

Suddenly the car started to shake from side to side and a crescendo of raised Irish voices told us the spectators had arrived! There were scores of them – I had no idea where they'd all come from! They were all shouting instructions but not listening to each other. Some were pushing while others were pulling and chaos reigned, with bits of the car being torn off in their efforts to get us back onto the road.

"Mike, get out and organise them.......you must ORGANISE them!" Pentti shouted.

I climbed out and tried to create some sense of co-ordinated action from our willing friends. Unfortunately, it didn't work and they were mortified that their valiant efforts had failed to see us on our way and drowned their sorrows with cans of Guinness. After the stage was closed they finally managed to pull us back onto the road, with the assistance of a very old and very smoky Land Rover. After a couple of miles, however, the Chevette's engine let go with a loud bang. The car had spent so much time in a vertical position on the river bed that the oil had siphoned out of the engine and, starved of lubricant, it seized. Not only were we out of the rally, but now we had no working engine to get us back to Belfast! For me, it was a sad end to a rather strange rally.

However, some of our spectator 'friends' were not finished with us! Four of them had been following us in their old, and rather battered, Morris Marina. They saw our predicament and offered to give us a tow. Pentti fancied a visit to a decent night club, so they agreed to take us to a hotel in Dublin, then collect us the next morning and tow us back to Belfast! We called the team on the radio, told them of our arrangement and released our service crew to support Jimmy, who was still leading the event. We met with one of the chase cars and collected our overnight bags.

The night club was called Mr. Bojangles in central Dublin and I vaguely remember some lovely Irish ladies trying to persuade us to buy their company with champagne and cigarettes at vastly inflated prices. We had little money with us, so we were quickly dropped as being of little or no value to them!

The next morning, our newly appointed 'service crew' arrived at our hotel, as promised, in their bright yellow hand-painted Marina. They had brought a new tow rope with them - the one used on the previous night had been a bit on the short side. This new rope was much longer, too long in fact, but they didn't want to cut it, so we set off, now travelling some considerable distance behind our tow car and into what was to be a most hilarious journey to Belfast. We had no way of communicating with the lads in the Marina who, it turned out, were not familiar with Dublin. They often forgot we were there as they went the wrong way around roundabouts and the wrong way down a one-way street. We could do nothing but sit behind them, helpless and in tears of laughter, and go wherever they took us!

At one point we even set off down the wrong side of a dual carriageway. It took them a few hundred yards to realise their mistake and they carried out a swift u-turn. This was fine for the Marina but the steering lock on the Chevette was such that we couldn't make the manoeuvre in one attempt. So, three of the lads jumped out and pushed us back to enable our three-point turn to be completed, accompanied by much horn-blowing and shouts of abuse from other road users. Unabashed, they gave us a big grin and a thumbs up and we set off again at considerable speed. They were fantastic lads and loving every minute of their time towing a super-star rally driver and his rally car behind them. However, the journey was not without its dangers. On several occasions they pulled out to overtake slower vehicles and misjudged the performance of their underpowered engine, just pulling back in time to avoid traffic coming the other way. Unfortunately, this left us still alongside the vehicle being overtaken and facing head-on to oncoming traffic! It was absolutely hilarious and we laughed until our sides hurt.

Miraculously, we arrived in Belfast in one piece. We parked the 'dead' Chevette in the hotel car park and took the four lads out for a well-deserved meal. They flatly refused any payment for fuel costs, insisting they'd had the best time of their lives. Irish rally spectators are the salt of the earth!

Russell Brookes finally won the rally with our team-mate Jimmy McRae finishing second, having lost the lead after spending time off the road. Markku Alen completed the podium in third place.

The Welsh International was to be a particularly tough rally as usual, covering 250 stage miles. Pentti had won the event the previous year so we were seeded Number 1. There had been some enforced changes to our Chevette following the Circuit of Ireland Rally. It was deemed that our Lotus designed 16 valve cylinder head was not legal, and we had to revert to the older Vauxhall designed head. There had been no time to develop this and we were faced with a considerable drop in power over the Welsh stages. Pentti drove as hard as he could but we were not particularly competitive, never lying higher than fifth overall.

We were gelling well as a crew and driving the underpowered car up to, and occasionally beyond, its limit! Back on the familiar forest stages, I was once more reading the roads from the OS maps. We arrived at the Dyfnant Forest stage and, while we waited for our time, I told Pentti about the stage:

"From the start Pentti, it's one hundred yards to a ninety left and ninety right. Then it's absolutely straight for point eight of a mile over a series of blind crests, all of them flat. You will see the end of the straight - it's where the trees are directly ahead of you at a tee junction."

"Ah," he said, "this is good. This is vy I like an English co-driver in the forests."

We set off around the left and right bends and onto the straight. Going through the gears we arrived at the first crest.

"Straight," I said and we flew over the crest flat out. Soon we were up into fifth gear and really motoring as we approached the next blind crest.

"Straight," I ordered. We continued, still flat out. The next crest came up.

"Straight," I repeated one more time.

We crested the brow at well over a hundred miles an hour........to see the old road straight ahead, just as I had promised, but now full of blown up tree stumps and with a new road cut off to the right at 45 degrees. I have never seen such reactions. Pentti flung the car sideways one way, and then the other, desperately trying to scrub off speed. We went into the ditch on the left hand side, cut the apex on the inside of the corner, up onto two wheels and ran wide into the outside ditch on the exit! We just, and I do mean just, got round the bend. When we reached the end of the stage I thought I had better say something:

"Pentti, I'm sorry, but they have changed the stage."

"Vot?" he asked. "Oh, don't vorry, ve save at least ten seconds there!" Several following competitors were to end their rally down the old road, having crashed into the blown up tree stumps!

Later in the event we arrived for the start of the long Dovey Forest stage, still lying fifth overall. I received our start time and, after the countdown, Pentti dropped the clutch. The car shot forward a few feet and promptly stopped - the engine had died! After a minute of trying, it fired up again, so we rolled back and I cheekily asked the marshal for another start time. This is strictly not allowed and I wasn't expecting one but, to my surprise, he obliged! The car stalled again and, amazingly, I managed to get a third start time, much to the dismay of the following competitors, who would, no doubt, have protested if we had successfully continued. However, it was all to no avail as the Chevette refused to move further than 50 yards, so we switched everything off and retired.

Our service crew arrived after the stage had closed and we were mortified to find that the car started and ran perfectly. We were all rather confused by this, but the source of the problem came to light when I switched the Terratrip back on and the engine promptly stopped again! The navigation unit was somehow interfering with the car's electronic ignition system, causing it to fail. It was hugely frustrating.

The event was eventually won by the all conquering Hannu Mikkola.

We travelled north in June for the fabulous Scottish Rally. I loved the Scottish - its forest stages were awesome, if somewhat rough and very dusty in dry weather. The Scottish scenery is to die for, not that we got too much time to see it! The rally was held over four days throughout a very large part of Scotland and consisted of some 40 special stages, totalling around 275 stage miles. There was the usual crop of rallying super-stars in the entry list. Our engine power had, by now, been restored to normal levels and we were feeling pretty confident of achieving a good result.

Our main opposition was Hannu Mikkola and, right from the start, he powered ahead. Our teammate, Jimmy McRae, hit a tree on the first stage and drove a banana-shaped Chevette throughout the rest of the rally. For some reason, Pentti was rather subdued from the start and we were lying in sixth place after day one. I was a bit perplexed but, not wanting to add to the problem, I kept quiet. Nevertheless, at the end of the penultimate day, after we had continued to slide down the order, I felt I had to say something because we were down to eighth.

"Pentti, are you OK?" I tentatively enquired.

"Yes, vy?" he asked.

"It's just that, if we go on like this, we are likely to finish outside the top ten."

"Listen," he said, "I promise you ve vill not finish outside the top ten.......ve might not finish, but ve vill not finish outside the top ten!"

True to his word we didn't. In fact he drove some of the best stages I had ever witnessed with him at the wheel and we charged back up the leader board.

On a particularly fast and very rough stage in Inchnacardoch Forest we lost our brakes yet again - it was rapidly becoming the Chevette's Achilles heel. Naturally, in spite of my suggestion to do so, Pentti refused to slow down. I was protesting that we really needed to finish the rally and at that point we were in a secure second overall behind the seemingly invincible Mikkola, with only a handful of stages to go.

"It's OK, it's OK!" comforted Pentti, as we charged through the stage at unreduced speed.

"I've said it before, you vorry too much!"

I considered reminding him about our Circuit of Ireland 'off' in similar circumstances but decided to bite my lip. However, things were becoming pretty wild and on one tightening downhill left-hand corner, with a big drop off to the outside, the car was scrubbing off speed and getting more and more sideways as it veered towards the drop.

Halfway through this lurid manoeuvre, with his left hand on the wheel and on full opposite lock, he elbowed me with his free arm shouting: "You like this, yeah, you like this!" I wasn't sure if it was a question or an instruction! He roared with laughter but I didn't find it particularly funny. Nevertheless, we somehow survived the moment, and went on to finish second behind Mikkola.

Blydenstein Racing was owned by the famous, ex-racing driver, Bill Blydenstein and his wife Frances Mary. Bill was not a rally enthusiast and never ventured out on events. However, on this occasion, he decided to come along to the Scottish Rally to see for himself what it was all about - rallying was paying his mortgage and he was prepared to put up with it. On the last day he decided to spectate and went to a stage that is well-known for being extremely rough and strewn with boulders. Believe it or not, this was the first stage he had ever seen live!

Pentti was back on form again and we absolutely flew over the last few stages as we climbed back up the leaderboard, including the one where Bill was watching. We came past at high speed and very sideways, the engine pulling maximum revs and the car crashing its way across the rocks. Bill almost fainted! He had no idea of the extent of punishment rally cars were subjected to on a stage and was mortified at the treatment being meted out to his beautiful Chevette! At the end of the rally, he came across and spoke to us:

"Do you really have to drive quite so fast over the rougher stages?" he asked. "It destroys the underside of my cars!" I don't think Bill ever fully grasped the idea behind rallying!

Pentti and I were entered on the Castrol 78 National Rally, a one-day forest event in central Wales starting from Aberystwyth, as a shakedown for the impending RAC Rally. Ari Vatanen had the same idea and brought along an Escort, as did Bjorn Waldegard. The battle for the rally was, of course, between our Chevette and the two Escorts, and it was very close all day. There were just seven long stages in Dovey and Hafren Forests, totalling some 100 stage miles.

Ari was marginally quicker than us and led the event from the start. Waldegard lost time off the road and dropped out of contention. Then, Ari's Escort broke its gear-linkage, the distraction causing the Finn to lose a few seconds down a firebreak! That allowed us through to lead the event, though our lead was trimmed back when we suffered a puncture. It was very tense and, in the end, we just hung on to win by fourteen seconds. It looked like it would be a close battle on the RAC.

The 1978 RAC Rally was to be my last event co-driving for Airikkala. For the following year it was planned for him to compete in a number of foreign pace note events, as well as the British Championship. Fellow Finn, Risto Virtanen, would be joining the team to co-drive for him and I was to move across to the sister car with Jimmy McRae. Nevertheless, this last rally with Pentti turned out to be pretty memorable for a number of reasons!

Just prior to the event it was arranged for the BBC's celebrated commentator, Harry Carpenter, to be driven by Pentti around the Bagshot military training grounds in our RAC Rally Chevette. There followed an unforgettable broadcast on BBC Grandstand, with Harry screaming into the microphone as he was subjected to Pentti's driving in very snowy conditions. This remains a classic piece of television, repeated many times over the following years.

The start was in Birmingham and, as with other RAC Rallies of the time, it was a tough event on both car and crew. It consisted of a 2000 mile slog around much of the British Isles over four days, with no less than 76 special stages, totalling over 500 stage miles, in the UK's best forests, and with most of the stages held in darkness.

The first day's stages were mainly aimed at spectators and were generally referred to by competitors as 'Mickey Mouse' stages. They were, however, quite capable of ruining one's rally if not treated with some respect. One such stage was Donington Park, where tens of thousands of spectators turned out to watch. We arrived running fourth on the road, lying fourth overall and set off into the stage. This was a mixture of tarmac circuit and some infield loose surface tracks. We finished the stage but the Chevette's gearbox was playing up. It was decided that we would take no chances and, at the service area in the Donington paddock, the mechanics set about changing it. This took around twenty minutes. I was anxious to get moving because the next stage was in Clipstone Forest near Mansfield, where every car that passed through ahead of us would cut up the sandy surface and make competitive times more difficult to achieve. In those days we were allowed to make up lost time on the subsequent road section, so we left at high speed to try and recover some of our lateness - it was dark by now.

We joined the M1 Motorway north-bound and Pentti sat in the fast lane with the engine at its maximum 8500rpm. On the forest gearing this was a true 119mph. After a few minutes Pentti's voice came over the intercom:

"Mike, how much further on motorway?"

I checked the trip-meter.

"Twelve miles, Pentti."

"OK," came the reply. A little while later came the same question:

"Mike, how much further on motorway?"

"Er, four miles, why?"

"Oh," said Pentti, "look behind!"

I turned and saw blue flashing lights a hundred yards or so behind us.

"Bugger! How long has he been there?" I asked my somewhat rattled driver.

"Oh, all the vay from Donington!"

I panicked!

"Bloody hell mate, you'll have to pull over or

he'll have us out the rally!"

Pentti duly obliged and the Granada police car pulled up in front of us on the hard shoulder. A very large and burly Sergeant got out of the car (it turned out he was Welsh). He stormed towards us, obviously very angry, not least because it had taken him some sixteen miles to finally get us to stop! We were in a British registered Vauxhall Chevette, so our not so friendly policeman assumed it was right-hand drive. He approached my side of the car and ripped the door open.

"You speak no English!" Pentti instructed over the intercom. I was happy to oblige!

"What the bloody hell do you think you are doing?" the policeman demanded.

"Er....erm, no speak English," I replied, trying to sound Scandinavian and pointed to Pentti. He slammed the door and rushed around to Pentti's side, virtually tearing his door off its hinges.

"What the bloody hell do you think you are doing?" he demanded, more frustrated than ever. Pentti rattled off a few words in Finnish and then said slowly:

"I....speak....no....English."

The policeman was beside himself with anger,

bright red in the face and furiously poking Pentti in the chest as he roared:

"I want to know, why you were doing a hundred and twenty miles an hour on the M1?"

There was a pause then Pentti replied....."Cos it vouldn't go any faster!!"

The sergeant was virtually speechless with rage. In the end all he could do was draw '70' pictures in the air with his hand!

"Seventy," he shouted, "you are only allowed seventy, now piss off!"

We continued at the obligatory speed limit, rather chastened, and with the police car following us to the Clipstone stage start.

Kielder Forest saw our retirement as, coincidentally, it did for both of the other Chevettes on the event. Our team-mate, Jimmy McRae, slid off the road and was unable to continue, while the works supported Chevette of Chris Sclater retired with electrical problems.

We had been in full flow on one of the longer Kielder stages when the oil pressure warning light illuminated. That's never good news, so Pentti switched off the engine immediately and we coasted to a halt at the side of the forest track. We were right in the middle of the Kielder complex, seemingly miles from civilisation and it was very dark. Shining a torch under the bonnet, we could immediately see the problem - the oil pump drive had failed. The Chevette had a rather strange system for holding the pulley onto the oil pump shaft – it was held in place by a series of Allen screws, which had loosened off enough to allow the pulley to spin without driving the pump.

We suddenly became aware that there was someone standing beside us. Startled, we looked up and saw an old farmer looking under the bonnet with us! We were miles from anywhere - where the hell had he come from?

"What you need there boys is a set of Allen keys," said the old chap.

"Yeah, yeah," retorted Pentti, "ve know that, thank you very much."

The old boy rummaged through his pocket and triumphantly pulled out...........a set of Allen keys! What on earth was he doing with a set of Allen keys? Did he carry them with him all the time just in case a rally car needed them?

Pentti grabbed the keys, found the correct size, and tried to tighten the screws. Sadly, the old chap's key was so badly corroded, it broke. It was an amazing coincidence though - miles from anywhere, this old chap just happened to have exactly the tool we needed, though unfortunately it did not retrieve the situation and we were out of the rally.

Thus ended my year co-driving for Pentti - it had been a strange one in many ways. Pentti was a hugely talented and ultra-quick rally driver and, for much of the time, he was on lightning form.

He was a rather complex character and I never really understood his mood swings. Most of the time it was great to be in his company and he had a good sense of humour (for a Finn!). When he was in this mood his driving was incredible. However, as I had witnessed on both the Circuit of Ireland and the Scottish Rally, his demeanour could rapidly change and his driving would suffer.

Some years later he moved to a magnificent house on the banks of the Thames in Maidenhead, which he bought from Sheila Ferguson, lead singer of the Three Degrees. His neighbours were Michael Parkinson and Rolf Harris. He had long retired from rallying but was promoting his left-foot braking school and invited me down for lunch.

He kept a beautifully restored slipper launch at the bottom of the garden, the sister boat to Michael Parkinson's identical version. We went for a run up the Thames and pulled in for lunch at the famous Waterside Inn at Bray. The restaurant had its own pontoon and, as we came alongside, a couple of waiters ran down to take our ropes. It was the only way to arrive and we dined in style! Alan Sugar was eating at the next table and acknowledged Pentti with a nod and a smile. It was a memorable experience for me, not being used to such rich pleasures.

Pentti is, sadly, no longer on this earth and is probably up there somewhere teaching 'Piggy' and 'Mad Dan' how to left-foot brake!

During the year I'd had the opportunity to meet some senior people from Vauxhall Motors, including the Marketing Director, the Fleet Sales Director and the Managing Director. I was pretty bored working in the food industry and was very keen to join Vauxhall in a sales or marketing role and I pushed them pretty mercilessly for a job! Although I was being paid for my rallying activities, co-drivers in those days didn't earn enough to cover all the household bills and the mortgage. The expense of feeding a young family was considerable and it was necessary to hold down a 'proper' job as well.

I was asked to travel to Luton for a formal interview with John Butterfield, the Fleet Sales Director. He told me of plans to set up a new Fleet Sales Division, including a National Fleet sales force and hinted that I may be offered a role if I was interested. I was very keen and he promised he would be in touch. It would be a perfect move for me as there was an implication that reasonable time off for my Vauxhall rallying 'duties' would not be a problem. I waited for a further call but I would be waiting for a considerable time.

JIMMY McRAE

While the 1979 British Rally Championship remained hugely popular, it was not a memorable year as far as I was concerned. The entry list read like the who's who of rallying and included Stig Blomqvist, Per Eklund, Henri Toivonen, Hannu Mikkola, Jochi Kleint, Timo Salonen, Markku Alen, Bjorn Waldegard, Jean-Pierre Nicolas and the usual crop of top UK drivers.

I had switched Chevettes within Dealer Team Vauxhall to co-drive for Jimmy McRae. Jim had been our team-mate during the previous year, when I was with Pentti, and he was a breath of fresh air, being affable, level-headed (most of the time!) and great to be around. Fiercely patriotic, he would take every opportunity on long road sections to lecture me on the appalling treatment of the Scots by various English kings over previous centuries. I'm sure, however, that some of his tales were suitably enhanced to emphasise his cause! I eventually got to know quite a lot about the history of Scotland and the Scottish struggle over the years, and I enjoyed his company immensely.

It became obvious in the early part of the year that Jim and I would be very much the number two crew in the Vauxhall Team. Pentti was always first in line for any development parts and we would only get them for our car when, or even if, they became available.

During the year Jim and I were dove-tailing the National Rally Championship between the events of the more senior British Open Series. This gave us a second opportunity for success. We contested this national series using a single-cam Chevette prepared by the SMT Group in Scotland. This light and nimble car was, at 170bhp, considerably less powerful than its bigger sister but it was really fantastic in the forests. It could be thrown into any corner at almost any speed and it would come out the other side begging for more! We loved it and had considerable success with the car, winning several events.

However, we had a few problems on one event in Wales when the rear axle locating mounts broke away from the body while we were leading the rally, which allowed the whole axle to move. We made it to the service area where our two mechanics, the ever reliable Alex Strathdee and Ian Anderson, rigged up a temporary repair for the last three short forest stages using chains and ropes. They asked if they could roll a few minutes into our lateness to finish the job properly and, as the event was nearly over, I agreed. We eventually booked into the 'Service Out' control three minutes late. I was angry with myself when I later found that, unusually, this was the only service area on the event where there was no penalty-free lateness allowed, and the three minutes were added to our stage times! This dropped us from first to third overall. I felt pretty bad about it but, it has to be said, that without the extra three minutes to complete the repair, it was doubtful whether we would have finished the rally at all. A guaranteed third overall was better than a non-finish and by the end of the year it made no difference to the Championship results.

Jim once commented on co-drivers making the occasional mistake (and most of us made very few): "I make five mistakes on every special stage and no-one knows about them, but if a co-driver makes one single mistake, the whole world hears about it." That's very true.

The little Chevette did us proud throughout the year - it was a fabulous rally car.

In the meantime, I was still waiting for the phone call from the Vauxhall Motors Fleet Boss confirming my new fleet sales role but, unfortunately, I learned that the proposed programme had been put on hold. It was very frustrating.

The Mintex Rally was our first Open Championship event together. I got on really well with Jim, instantly gelling with him in the car. Yorkshire had seen a lot of snow in the run up to the event and many of the stages were blocked by competitors going off and becoming completely stuck. Two or three others would then arrive and help remove the stricken car. A queue would form, leading to lines of rally cars following each other through the stage. The second car in the queue would become frustrated by the pace of the first car and try to pass – then that would go off in the process and become firmly wedged in a snow bank, causing yet more delays. There was no penalty relief for those crews caught up in these situations and many minutes were lost. It was complete chaos! Pentti retired very early with engine problems and we lost considerable time due to other people's accidents and blocked stages, eventually finishing a lowly eleventh. It was not a great start to our campaign.

The Circuit of Ireland Rally wasn't much kinder to us. Once again there was a bumper entry of rallying stars for this mammoth event, which took place over no less than 630 stage miles. There was considerable carnage, with Tony Pond and Russell Brookes crashing out in the early stages. A warning board had been wrongly placed in advance of a small jump, when it should have been a few hundred yards further along the stage and warning of a huge jump! Both cars were seriously damaged in the 'crash-landing' and both retired from the rally on the spot. We soldiered on, doing OK but nothing more, and managed to creep up to fifth overall. This was as high up the leaderboard as we managed, for the clutch failed soon afterwards and we retired. The consolation for Vauxhall was that Pentti won the event after a superb drive.

The Welsh was equally unmemorable! The event was very wet, very windy and the stages were extremely slippery. Hannu Mikkola returned to the Championship in scintillating form and simply drove his Escort away from the rest of the field. Nobody could get near him.

Our number two status in the team was highlighted when we arrived at the Cardiff start to be told that Pentti was not happy with his engine and there would be a swap. He was to take our engine and we were to run his 'duff' one! We were pretty unhappy about it, but 'c'est la vie' when you are number two in a team. The engines were duly swapped. I have to say that we didn't think there was anything wrong with the supposedly 'duff' engine, but we were not really on top form and rather struggled on the event, lying just inside the top ten. I must also admit that we were not exactly devastated when our team leader retired his Chevette on the Epynt stages with engine problems! In fact, I'm sure we enjoyed a little chuckle at his expense! As I said, 'c'est la vie'!

We carried on, with niggling electrical problems slowing our progress, to finish a relatively poor seventh overall. Not a great result and we were not particularly happy!

The Scottish Rally, Jimmy's home event, was again a bit up and down for us. We had some good battles, lying fifth for much of the event, rising to fourth after Timo Salonen's Fiat 131 differential seized. Sadly, mechanical gremlins struck again and our rather unreliable Chevette ground to a halt.

The battle for the lead between Airikkala and Pond finally went our team-mate's way when Pond's Sunbeam Lotus suffered a blown engine.

I still hadn't received word from Vauxhall about any new job and my current employer was becoming pretty inflexible about my taking time off for rallying activities. Because of this I had to decline co-driving for Jim on the Ulster Rally. It was hugely frustrating especially as he went on to finish an excellent second overall.

September brought the Manx Rally and I was back in the Chevette's left-hand seat. Surely our luck would return on this fantastic tarmac event. Jim and I spent a considerable amount of time refining our pace notes to give us the best possible chance of turning our season around. It started well and, after the first day, we were second overall behind Tony Pond's Sunbeam Lotus.

Airikkala crashed out early on in the event and life was sweet! Unfortunately, we lost some time on the night stages when an oil leak from the axle contaminated the rear tyres. We had a couple of very wild moments, eventually having to slow down until it was fixed at service. This let Brookes through and, when Tony Pond retired with mechanical problems, it left a straight fight between ourselves and Russell, who was by now some thirty seconds ahead. We were slowly gaining on him, stage by stage, a couple of seconds here and a couple there when, without warning, the gear lever popped out of its socket! Retrieving it from the floor, I replaced it and, using both hands, held it in position while Jim changed gear, steered the car and turned the pace note pages! Obviously, this was not conducive to particularly safe or quick driving and, after a couple of scares, we decided to call it quits and settle for second place behind Russell. At least we had achieved a half-decent result.

We finished the 1979 season with an incident free twelfth overall on the RAC Rally, ending what was, frankly, a pretty average season. As I mentioned earlier, we were very pleased to have achieved considerable success during the year in the National Series with the SMT Chevette - it saved our year!

I had really enjoyed my first year co-driving for Jimmy. We'd had limited success in the Open Championship and we looked forward to something rather better in 1980. This would almost certainly be helped by the fact that Airikkala had moved on from the British Rally Championship scene for a programme of selected World Championship events. This left us at the forefront of Vauxhall's British Open Championship challenge and we took to the task with increased confidence that we would have the full support of the team's management and more reliable machinery. Certainly there would be no-one to steal our engines!

For the coming year we were to campaign the newly developed Chevette HSR, which enjoyed several improvements over the old HS model, not least an increased track for better handling. These changes, however, were more evolution than revolution.

The Chevette was basically a great rally car – its handling, power, traction and agility were all first class and it had all the ingredients for a successful year. We just needed reliability and the full support of the Team to succeed and we were to enjoy much more of both.

AT LAST - A NEW JOB!

Shortly after the RAC Rally I received a phone call from John Butterfield's secretary at Vauxhall Motors, asking me to go down to Luton for a further meeting. John was the Fleet Sales Director who had interviewed me sometime before. I had more or less forgotten about the proposed new role, having heard nothing for over a year and had presumed that the new division had been canned. John was one of the nicest guys you could wish to meet and I was over the moon when he told me that the new Fleet Team was, at last, to be set up in early 1980 and I was to be part of it. He apologised for the delay and put it down to the normal General Motors 'treacle'. I received all the paperwork, hurriedly resigned from the Imperial Group, and took up my new role as Fleet Account Manager for the North of England. Vauxhall was planning to launch the new front-wheel drive

Cavalier a few months later and, to be honest, when it was introduced to the market, selling these 'advanced' cars to major fleet operators was a doddle.

HE WAS A BILLY COLEMAN FAN!

The first Open Championship event of 1980 was, as usual, the Mintex Rally which, this particular year, started from Newcastle upon Tyne. It was a punishing event consisting of 50 special stages, mostly held in the fabulous forests of Yorkshire. Again the entry list included the cream of the crop, with the familiar faces of Vatanen, Toivonen, Mikkola, Eklund, Blomqvist, Pond, Brookes and, for the first time, the Swede, Anders Kullang, in the all new Opel Ascona 400.

Conditions on the first day and night were truly awful. The stages were wet, muddy, extremely slippery and, just to make things more difficult, they were covered in thick fog.

Retirements came thick and fast. Kullang's new Opel stopped with mechanical failure as early as stage two. However, the fog did rather play into our hands. Many of the UK co-drivers were pretty adept at reading the forest roads from the (mainly!) accurate OS maps of the area, giving our drivers an advantage in the poor visibility. This came to the attention of several Finns, including Henri Toivonen, who vociferously claimed that it was cheating! Reading the maps in thick fog, while the driver is travelling at a much higher speed than would otherwise be safe was, nevertheless, a pretty daunting experience for both co-driver and driver alike, but it usually paid off.

We ended the first night in a trouble-free fifth overall and the following day, once the fog had lifted, we really put the hammer down, climbing the leaderboard to finish third overall behind Mikkola and Vatanen. We were pretty pleased with our first result of the year.

Easter came and it was time for the Circuit of Ireland. Many of the competitors, including ourselves, were staying at the Europa Hotel in Belfast, famous at the time for being the most bombed hotel in the world! The Scandinavian drivers were somewhat nervous of a terrorist attack and, with the rally being such a high profile event, it seemed a perfect target. This gave us an opportunity to wind them up. We told them that the only way to stay safe was to remove the mattress from their beds, sleep on the base and put the mattress on top of them. Then, if there was a bomb, the mattress would shield them from the shards of flying glass. It was a bit cruel, I suppose, but any advantage had to be taken! There were a few Scandinavians seen with sore backs over the next few days!

During one afternoon, prior to the rally start, Belfast was subjected to a really horrendous thunderstorm of continental proportions. I was watching out of my bedroom window when there was a huge crash of thunder and a simultaneous brilliant flash of lightning – it was so close I actually heard the lightning 'fizz'. This set off the hotel alarms. One of our Scandinavian competitor friends, who I will not name (though many will be able to guess his identity!), was asleep in his bedroom and thought it was a bomb. He ran into the corridor, down the fire escape and out into the street below. He was completely naked and stood there shivering in front of bemused shoppers! Boy, did we enjoy that – he was ribbed mercilessly!

Jim was on top form and we were leading the event as we crossed the border into the Republic of Ireland. Billy Coleman, the idol of Irish rallying, was hot on our heels in his Escort but we were relatively comfortable and not really stretching the Chevette. However, on a stage near Dundalk everything went pear-shaped for us. The car hit a deep pothole on the inside of a corner which wrenched the steering wheel out of Jim's hand. We lurched to the right and, before it could be brought back under control, the car ran up a bank, through a hedge and rolled over into the adjacent field. The Chevette was a bit of a mess, many of the body panels were bent and several windows lost. However, it landed back on its wheels so I jumped out to open a gate to allow us to rejoin the road. Just as I was doing this, Billy Coleman, running next on the stage, came round the corner sideways. I thought I'd better let him know we were OK and I gave him the thumbs up. This distracted the Irishman who stared and promptly did a wall of death act on the outside of the next right-hand bend! Luckily, he got away with it.

For the rest of the day we had to endure the rude gestures and jeers of the many Coleman fans that lined the stages as they spotted our battered Chevette! This 'shunt' cost us the lead, which Coleman inherited, only for his Escort to retire sometime after with a blown engine. Ari Vatanen was then promoted to the number one position, with us close behind in second place. Our car was a bit of a mess but the service lads did their usual great job of tidying it up, using copious amounts of duct tape.

The only part of the car that wasn't damaged in the roll was my door, but this was put right soon afterwards! We were driving slowly through a village and stopped at a tee junction. There was an old chap standing on the pavement wearing gaiters and hob-nailed boots. For some reason he ran towards us and landed a well-aimed kick on my door, putting a large dent in it. We assumed he was a Billy Coleman fan!

Then one of the greatest battles ever witnessed on a rally commenced. Both Jim and Ari were right on the ragged edge as we tackled the classic stages of the Republic of Ireland. Sunday's run around the Ring of Kerry included two of the best stages in the world, Moll's Gap and Tim Healey Pass, and it was a privilege to be part of the fight, even though it was pretty scary at times. We gradually clawed back some of the time, a couple of seconds here, a couple there, and arrived back in Killarney in the late afternoon just eighteen seconds behind Ari. It was exhausting stuff and we looked forward to a good rest before the noon start of the last leg on the following day. The Rally HQ in Killarney was based at the Great Southern Hotel in the town centre and we walked down in the evening for a pint of Guinness. We set off to return to our hotel at about ten o'clock to find it was absolutely bucketing down with rain. We were preparing to get soaked when a broad Irish voice shouted: "Jimmy, can I give you a lift?"

We accepted the kind offer and our Irish friend fetched his car, a very old 105E Anglia. He opened the door, pushed the seat forward for me to climb into the back and started lashing out at something inside. There were two chickens on the back seat, clucking furiously in protest as they were made to shift to allow me to get in. The rear seat was completely covered in chicken 'droppings' so I had to crouch, rather than sit, for the one mile journey. Only in Ireland!

The fight with Vatanen re-commenced in earnest the following day. We had to fix a brake problem on the road section to the first stage and very nearly ran into time penalties, which would have ended the fight there and then. However, we just made the stage start in time, arriving with seconds to spare and with brakes and tyres fully up to operating temperature! It was exhilarating stuff, the two drivers wringing the necks of the Chevette and the Escort and driving way over any sensible maximum. With no pace notes allowed on the Circuit it was down to the 'Mk1 eyeball' to follow the road ahead and look for danger.

Ari was determined to hang on to his first place and our progress towards him was slow, though we were gradually reducing the deficit, second by second. However, we were running out of time to catch him and, as we entered the stages on the last night, we decided to throw all caution to the wind. Jim was on fire! It was a joy to behold such fabulous driving first hand. One of the last stages of the rally contained a long and very fast straight. Charging down this straight, flat out, at somewhere around 100mph, we hit a series of very large bumps. The car took off, landed with a crash and launched into a huge 'tank slapper' which we only just survived. By the time Jim had sorted it all out we were down to about 30mph! Boy, it was close and Jim had worked a miracle to keep it all together. We had used up our ninth life, however, and he reluctantly announced: "That's it, we'll settle for second!" Somewhat relieved, I agreed and we continued the stage at a slightly reduced pace.

Then, in the distance, we saw tail lights. It was nothing unusual when rallying in Ireland to occasionally come across a local car on the stages, especially in the small hours of the morning when a farm-hand was going to milk the cows. As we approached we could not believe what we were seeing. It was Ari Vatanen's Escort, badly bent and travelling slowly. He had hit the same bumps but hadn't been able to save the situation and had rolled, seriously damaging the steering. With front wheels splayed he could no longer fight, and it was with considerable delight that we passed him to lead the rally back into Belfast. It was a fantastic win and one of the toughest rallying battles I had ever been involved in. It was also hugely satisfying and we celebrated long into the night!

The 1980 Welsh Rally was not going to be so kind to us. We arrived leading the Championship, just three points ahead of Vatanen and eight points ahead of Mikkola. We were quite comfortable during the event, sitting just behind the two other Championship protagonists, who were having a massive battle at the head of the rally. Vatanen, for once, had the upper hand over his arch-rival. We reached the rest halt in Machynlleth on the second night suffering from a rather down on power engine - something was wrong. We retired to bed at 2.00am for a couple of hours of much needed sleep. Two hours later the Team boss, Gerry Johnstone, came to our room to tell us it was all over. The engine had incurred some serious internal damage and it wasn't possible to continue. Disappointment was tinged with some relief as we turned over and went back to sleep.

McRAE TERRITORY

The Scottish Rally had several stages close to Jimmy's Lanarkshire home. This was, of course, 'McRae territory' and I was amused to see many notices announcing the fact placed at the side of the road and telling other competitors to beware! Reliability issues raised their heads again and we had the gearbox jam in first gear, necessitating a long and very slow crawl to the end of the Kirroughtree stage. Then the differential broke sending us off the road for ten minutes, and finally the replacement gearbox started playing up! Along with others, we were also plagued with many punctures. These problems led us to lose a considerable amount of time.

Hannu Mikkola took revenge for his Welsh defeat by Ari Vatanen and won, ahead of his Finnish rival. We soldiered on, trying to make up lost time but, in the end, we could only manage seventh overall, though still holding on to third place in the British Championship.

We felt very sorry for Russell Brookes, who finished the last stage in third place, only to have his engine expire on the road section to Aviemore. The head gasket had failed just a few road miles short of the finish line. The rally also saw a nasty accident for the young rising star, Malcolm Wilson, who went off on a high speed section, hitting a culvert, breaking both his ankles and ending up in hospital.

It was soon time to return to the Isle of Man for the fabulous Manx International. Once again we made a lot of effort during our practice period to perfect our notes. Competition would be tough, with Tony Pond and the mighty TR7 V8 tipped for the win.

As expected, Tony powered the TR7 into the lead from the very first stage, with us hanging on as best as we could in second place. When he was on form Pond was a hard man to beat and, with the V8's awesome power and the tarmac roads of the island suiting the low-slung TR7, he was in a league of his own. We had some problems with our intercom when it failed on the first stage which didn't help our cause. It wasn't possible to replace it until the first service after three stages, by which time I had virtually lost my voice from having to shout the notes. Then, on one of the night-time stages, the car suffered a split in an under-bonnet oil pipe which sprayed lubricant onto the windscreen, making life very difficult on the ultra high-speed stages. I was timing the pace notes by the 'feel' of the car due to the lack of forward visibility, while Jim was driving virtually blind!

During the night section Pond's TR7 suffered a puncture allowing us to pull into parc ferme ahead, but with a mere two second lead! We were not confident of staying ahead the next day and, inevitably, Pond used the V8's power to edge back in front. We thought we were heading for a well-earned second place, but it wasn't to be. First, the gearbox began playing up, with the subsequent gear-selection difficulties losing us time, then, more seriously, the distributor rotor arm failed, leaving the car stationary mid-stage. Luckily, we carried a spare in the car and we were able to replace it, though Jim's hand was quite badly burned by the hot engine exhaust in the process. I counted seven rally cars passing our stranded

Chevette and sure enough we had lost seven minutes exacting the repair. It was a shame, but at least we were back in the rally and charging back up the leaderboard, eventually finishing third overall. Pond's TR7 won the rally, with Vatanen's Escort second. It was a disappointment but at least we managed to hang on to finish third in the British Open Championship – a pleasing result for both ourselves and the team.

INTO THE LION'S DEN!

In the run up to the 1980 RAC Rally several team changes were announced for the following year. Jim McRae was to join Opel to campaign an Ascona 400, with Ian Grindrod joining him as co-driver. I was to stay with Vauxhall to sit alongside Tony Pond, who was joining us to drive the latest version of the Chevette HSR in the Open Championship.

I had thoroughly enjoyed my time with Jimmy and would leave with a much greater knowledge of Scottish history! The RAC Rally was due to be our last event together and I hoped it would be good for us, with Jimmy leaving on a high.

The 1980 event started from Bath and the rally was soon in the headlines on all the TV news channels. Tony Pond's TR7 had a much publicised accident, going off in the grounds of the Longleat stage and ending up in the Safari Park's lion enclosure, crashing into their feeding trough in the process. Luckily, for Tony and co-driver Fred Gallagher, the lions were safely locked away and they continued with a considerably re-shaped TR7.

We were having a steady run, holding fifth place for much of the rally. However, as we were leaving the service area in Hawick, prior to the long stages of the Kielder Forest complex, we tested the auxiliary lamps that had just been fitted. There was a 'thud' from somewhere inside the car and all the lamps went out! This would have left us with just two rather feeble headlights to illuminate the sixty or so miles of dark and wet Kielder stages - not an ideal situation! The service crew sprung into action. There was little time to make repairs and all they could manage by way of a fix was to hotwire the two long-range lamps through a switch. Illumination would be all or nothing but at least we would be able to see the road ahead.

We arrived at the first stage, a long twenty mile thrash through some of the UK's fastest forest roads. It was pouring with rain, as only it can in Kielder, the raindrops looking as long as stair-rods in the lights. We set off on the stage and it was a nightmare. With the spotlights on, the reflection off the rain was so bad it completely dazzled us but switching them off and relying on the headlights alone meant we couldn't see any distance ahead. At the end of one long straight there was a tightening left-hand bend which, with virtually no visibility, was impossible to see in time. The car ran wide and into the thick mud on the outside of the bend and was pulled into the ditch. We rolled at high speed, wrecking the car and finishing our rally on the spot. It was a very disappointing end to Jim's last drive in the Chevette.

THE LEGENDARY TONY POND

I was really looking forward to partnering Tony Pond again during 1981 and his arrival into the Vauxhall Team was greeted with much enthusiasm. He had been my British Leyland team-mate in 1977 when I was co-driving for Pat Ryan and I had taken part in the York National Rally with him, giving the TR7 its first win.

Tony was a great character, very easy to get on with and possessing a wicked (and sometimes cruel!) sense of humour. He had absolutely no 'side' to him, what you saw was what you got.

He was not only a highly successful rally driver but he was also a pretty good pilot. He once told me a story about a friend of his who had, for some time, been trying to persuade him to take him up in the Cessna 172 that he flew out of White Waltham airfield, near Maidenhead. Tony finally agreed, telling him that another acquaintance had also been begging him for a flight. It was arranged that they would all meet at the airfield one morning. They took off with his friend sitting in the back and the other 'acquaintance' sitting beside Tony in the front of the aircraft. After half an hour or so Tony announced that he was not feeling well and, without warning, passed out! The aircraft turned sharply to port and went into a spin. The guy in the front was panicking and turned round, frantically asking the fellow in the back what to do. The poor soul sitting behind was, by now, screaming like a child and weeping as he thought his life was about to end. The 'acquaintance' then suddenly grabbed the yoke and brought the aircraft back to level flight. Tony 'came round' crying with laughter. It had been a cruel hoax! The guy in the right-hand seat was actually a British Airways First Officer who flew the BAC 1-11 airliner in his day job. Tony was never forgiven and his friend never asked to fly with him again!

The first event of the year was again the Mintex Rally. Starting from Newcastle upon Tyne, the event ran through several stages on the Otterburn Military Ranges in the wilds of Northumberland. Here chaos reigned, with snow and ice causing mayhem. Cars were going off all over the place and, on the third stage, we joined them. A steep, uphill, tightening left-hand corner at the end of a long straight proved impossible to slow for and we went off on the sheet ice, becoming stuck in a ditch. We sat in the immovable Chevette and watched the rest of the field passing us. We also saw many returning, and running against the direction of the stage, after failing to climb a particularly steep section! We were eventually towed out and found that the organisers had cancelled stages four and five, considering them to be impassable. Most thought that stage three would follow suit because so many cars had been turning around and running the wrong way through the stage, which was totally against the regulations.

We had been officially excluded for being out of time but we continued under appeal while the stage three situation was sorted out. Tony wrung every bit of performance out of the Chevette on the rest of the rally and we finished the event at the top of the results. The organisers decided, in their wisdom, that the results of stage three would stand after all and we were once again excluded! Protests and appeals were flying back and forth and there was much debate as to the correct way to resolve the situation. There were even two sets of results posted at the finish while it was being sorted out! One set, with stage three results standing, showed Pentti Airikkala in his Escort as the winner; the other, with stage three cancelled, indicated that we had won! It was a complete mess but the organisers eventually stood firm, stage three results were confirmed, and we were finally excluded from the rally!

Pentti Airikkala was declared the winner, with Jimmy McRae finishing a fine second in the Opel. For us, though, it was a very frustrating end to a rather chaotic rally, especially as we'd been fastest on most of the stages and had nothing to show for it.

The Circuit of Ireland was our second outing together. It was a gruelling event with, again, over 600 miles of twisty and bumpy tarmac stages in its 1500 mile total. Over the Easter period it was hot, dry and dusty. Tony was really up for this one after our disappointment on the Mintex Rally and we powered into the lead from stage one. Early on, one of our main rivals, Airikkala, spun his Escort backwards into a tree causing serious damage to the rear bodywork and flattening the car's exhaust. The 'choked' engine refused to start until the pipe was opened up again and he lost considerable time, eventually retiring with further mechanical issues.

The stages south of the border were superb - fast and open, with mile after mile at very high speeds. It was still very much a time of the Irish 'troubles' and many competitors from the UK refused to take part for fear of being attacked. We never saw any problems during our years of taking part but occasionally something would remind us that trouble was not far away. I vividly remember powering down one stage near the town of Newry and seeing a chap standing at the side of the road. He had long black hair, a similar length beard, was extremely scruffy and wearing a rather shabby raincoat. As we approached he opened the raincoat in true 'flasher' style, but what he exposed rather shocked us – it was a Kalashnikov rifle! Without doubt, we were the fastest car down that particular straight, waiting for the inevitable shot. It never came or, at least if it did, he missed!

Tony and I continued to dominate the event, never truly extending ourselves and comfortably maintaining our lead, to head Jimmy McRae by fifty seconds at the end of the first leg. There was much carnage elsewhere, with cars off the road all over Ireland and many others suffering punctures and mechanical failure. This year's event was seemingly much harder on competitors than in previous years and, by the Killarney midway point, over 50 per cent of the entry list had retired.

Brookes went off in the Sunbeam Talbot Lotus on a fast right-hander, right in front of the TV cameras, losing several minutes and second place overall. Mike Broad, his co-driver, deserved an Oscar for milking the injury to his arm for the benefit of the viewers!

We had been in dominant form, not really pushing the Chevette too hard and maintaining a healthy lead over Jimmy McRae's Opel Ascona when, mid-stage, the gearbox shattered and left us stranded with no drive. We were out of the rally and suffered another disappointment. This left McRae in a comfortable lead, which he held to the end. It was not supposed to be like this and we were left hoping our luck would soon change!

Local Irish driver, Ger Buckley, upheld Vauxhall honours with an excellent second place in his privately entered Chevette HSR. A recovering

Russell Brookes clawed his way back to complete the podium in third place.

I loved these classic Circuit of Ireland rallies. The huge number of spectators and their all embracing enthusiasm for rallying had to be seen to be believed. Literally tens of thousands of them charged around Ireland at high speed following the event – it was just like Wacky Races!! Many were over exuberant and ended up in hospital after their inevitable accidents. One such incident still remains imprinted on my mind. We came over a crest on a road section and saw a yellow Ford Capri embedded in the top branches of a tree and some thirty feet off the ground! The driver had lost control, rolled and flipped the car high into the air, finishing with the car firmly lodged in the treetop. Luckily, the driver and passengers were unhurt and busily taking photographs of their mishap!

Soon it was May and we set off for Cardiff on our annual trip to the Welsh International Rally. The Welsh was still one of the most gruelling rallies on the calendar, covering a large part of Wales, virtually nonstop. Proper sleep was impossible, with the longest break being a mere two hours in the town of Machynlleth during the middle of the second night, where we had rooms booked in the Wynnstay Arms Hotel. Before taking a nap, we ordered some food from the overworked hotel staff, who were clearly not used to being up at two o'clock in the morning and were rather bad-tempered. I was starving, not having eaten properly for two days, and ordered a plate of Beef Bourguignon. It arrived and I was about to tuck in when Pond's droll tones announced: "My dog passed stuff like that last week. I had to take him to the vet!" As hungry as I was, I couldn't eat it and I retired for a couple of hours sleep!

The rally was going well and we were lying second overall, trailing Ari Vatanen's, Rothmans backed, Escort by a mere thirteen seconds.

Shortly after the restart the Finn's Escort punctured on the longer of the two Dovey stages, allowing us through into the lead. Unfortunately, this lead was destined to be short lived. In the middle of the night, tackling the Dyfnant Forest stage, we approached a crest at high speed. The gap in the trees, picked out by the lights, indicated that the road continued straight on and this was confirmed by arrows pointing straight ahead. We breasted the brow of the hill at full speed.........and charged straight down a firebreak! The road actually went 90 degrees left on the crest and the Welsh spectators, wanting to spice things up a little, had switched the arrows from indicating sharp left to pointing straight on just before we arrived! It worked, and we ended up some hundred yards up a firebreak and firmly stuck in the mud! I was pretty cross because the bend was clearly shown on the OS map that I was reading to Tony. I had hesitated, however, when I saw the arrows pointing straight on and realised the mistake only when it was too late to stop. I later checked with the car running in front of us and, at their time of passing, the arrows were correctly indicating a 90 left. Bastards!

The spectators did redeem themselves a little by pushing us out with the loss of only around a minute. In his effort to retrieve the car Tony over-revved the engine and bent the valve gear, causing some loss of power for the rest of the event. This 'off' dropped us down to third overall behind Vatanen and McRae, with just the tarmac Epynt Military stages to come. We started the first of these classic stages just eighteen seconds behind Jimmy, but he was determined not to let us through. Luckily for us, he suffered a puncture and second place was ours. With no chance of catching Vatanen's flying Escort we settled for a good second overall and a bagful of championship points.

My mother and father, God bless them, decided to hire a motor-home and surprise me by turning up during the event. Unfortunately, they became rather disorientated and never actually caught up with the rally! While we were driving up the finish ramp in Cardiff, they were still trying to find the rally in mid-Wales! I was quite upset, because if I had known their plans, I would have made sure that they had every detail needed to follow the event. They laughed about it afterwards!

Next, we travelled north of the border for the Scottish Rally. The event started in Glasgow and ran south through Eskdale and Craik Forests before heading north again overnight, taking in forest stages all the way to a rest halt in the Grampian ski resort of Aviemore. The final two days were to be run through some of the roughest stages in the UK before returning to Aviemore for the finish.

Leading up to the event we'd had discussions about other teams listening in to our radio transmissions, using scanners that were now available. Tony came up with a plan! We would list some of the problems we were likely to encounter during the event and give each one a reference number. Thus an engine problem would be reported over the radio as "number one", brakes "number two" and so on. In all, we had a comprehensive list of some twenty potential problems. The system would, unfortunately, turn out to be fallible!

Pentti Airikkala, with the rather inappropriately named 6 feet 6 inches Phil Short co-driving, was first off the Glasgow start ramp. On the first stage, Glentress - near the Border town of Peebles - we were immediately fastest. On the road section to the second stage we passed Airikkala's Rothmans Escort receiving some attention. We arrived at the second stage in the neighbouring Cardrona Forest and booked in at the arrival control. We were held back by the marshals as there was a short delay to the start of the stage, so we deliberately waited on a very narrow bridge. Airikkala arrived at speed with the horn blaring and booked in late, and on the same minute as ourselves. Phil Short was despatched to our window to ask if we would allow them to pass and run through the stage in front of us, which they had no entitlement to do.

"I've got to ask," he said, rather sheepishly, "but you won't let us pass, I suppose?" I think he already knew the answer!

"Nope!" replied Tony firmly.

His continued pleas fell on deaf ears and eventually poor old Phil trudged back to the car to be harangued by a raging Airikkala. I could imagine what Phil was going through having witnessed some of Pentti's rants first hand on the '78 Circuit of Ireland.

We eventually set off into the stage. Tony was absolutely flying and cutting all the corners, deliberately dislodging rocks and boulders, pulling them into the middle of the road, and into the path of the still furious Airikkala, who promptly punctured! He was absolutely thunderous at the next service area!

Tackling the Glen Errochty stage, just outside the tourist town of Pitlochry, our transmission woes struck again and the gearbox jammed in third gear, with a strong smell of hot transmission oil entering the car. Luckily, we were only three miles from the end of the stage.

"Get on the radio and tell the service crew." said Tony. "Tell them to have a new gearbox ready."

I rummaged through my bag trying to find the coded list of faults so that I could relay the problem and prevent any other competitor understanding our difficulty. I couldn't find it!

"What's the code for gearbox?" I asked.

"I'm f**ked if I know," said Pond, "you've got the list!"

I still couldn't lay my hands on it and by now we were nearing the end of the stage, so I gave up and alerted the lads over the radio in the old-fashioned way.

"The gearbox is knackered and we need a new one." I announced to the world!

Pond groaned in exasperation. We threw the list away after that!

Arriving at the end of the second leg in Aviemore, with no further dramas, we had built up a lead of just forty-seven seconds over arch-rival McRae. The stages were very rough and extremely slippery, catching out many competitors. Airikkala had spent several minutes off the road and had slipped out of contention, but Jim was hanging on to our shirt tails for all he was worth.

We started the last day in determined mood, this rally was going to be ours and nobody would prevent our victory! Jimmy had been telling everybody that he'd settled for second overall in order to 'bag' more British Championship points. We didn't believe him though, and continued flat out. Of course, it was Scottish gamesmanship, and he immediately took a few seconds off us on the first stage of the day!

Disaster nearly struck towards the end of the rally when, with just four stages to go, our steering rack broke away from the bulkhead. The car's handling was appalling and it was virtually undriveable on the road section to the service area. However, the mechanics did a fine job of a temporary repair in the fifteen minutes service time available. They simply drilled two new holes through the bulkhead and bolted the rack back on to it, using just one U-bolt! That was it! Just one flimsy U-bolt holding our steering together and with four of the roughest stages in Scotland to go!

We were holding a slender lead of just thirty seconds over McRae, so we couldn't back off. Jim was, I'm sure, aware of our problem now that our 'Enigma Code' had been discarded, and he put the hammer down. We had to put any thoughts of the inevitably huge accident that would result from steering failure out of our minds and continue flat out. It was nervy stuff, especially on the rougher sections. Miraculously, the temporary fix held together and we arrived back in Aviemore victorious and mightily relieved. Jimmy hadn't let up the pressure until two stages from the end, when he finally admitted defeat and backed off – we beat his Ascona by just over a minute, with Malcolm Wilson's Escort in third place.

Celebrations went on well into the night and I'm afraid we incurred the wrath of the Post House Hotel management. Post rally boredom had begun to set in as the adrenalin receded so, in the early hours of the morning, several drivers, co-drivers and other team members decided to create a special stage in the lounge area. Chairs, tables and stools were gathered from all over the hotel and placed close together around the outer walls. Competitors, most of whom were by now considerably worse for wear, were timed running the 'stage' over two laps. You were not allowed to touch the floor. There were numerous accidents but no serious injuries, although some of the hotel furniture looked a little second-hand the next morning and we all had to avoid the hotel staff who were looking for the guilty parties!

HEY, McRAE, VAINQUEUR!

Shortly after returning home from the Scottish I received a phone call from Jim McRae. The Opel Team had entered him and the Ascona 400 on the Switzerland based, Rallye du Vin. His regular partner, Ian Grindrod, was not available as he was competing in a World Championship event elsewhere, so Jim asked if I would be free to co-drive for him. The answer was a resounding, "Yes!"

We flew to Geneva and picked up a Kadett road car from GM Suisse for the restricted two day recce and proceeded to the rally base in the small town of Martigny. The Ascona arrived and the service crew set about preparing the car for the event, while we left to make pace notes for the stages. It was some rally! The stages were held over a mixed bag of surfaces. A typical stage would start on a minor tarmac road, turn onto farm tracks, back onto a main road and then turn into forestry land. Tyre choice was going to be very difficult indeed.

Many of the stages rose to a great height over the mountains and, during our first day of practice, we were in thick cloud for much of the time. On one very high section the road book showed a crest with a double-caution, leading to a 90 degree right-hand bend. In almost zero visibility we noted it carefully. The loose surface road then ran steeply downhill for some two miles to the stage finish.

On day two the sun was shining and under a clear blue sky we set off to check the notes we had made on the previous day, this time in good visibility. Arriving at the double-cautioned crest we were horrified to find that, should we fail to make the corner immediately afterwards, it would mean a 2000 feet drop, down a 60 degree slope, onto the ski resort of Verbier! The double caution was changed to a triple caution, the first time I had ever used such a note, but the corner was worthy of it! The steep downhill section, that followed immediately afterwards, also continued with a sheer drop on the co-driver's side (of course!) for the next couple of miles and did my vertigo no

A typical end of rally for the 'All-Aggro'!

At last, the Dolomite - 1976 Scottish Rally

Pat Ryan and the TR7 on the 1977 RAC Rally

Pentti in a jovial mood following our 1978 Mintex win

Pentti in full flow during the 1978 Scottish Rally - we were second to Mikkola!

With Jimmy McRae in the wonderful SMT single-cam Chevette

Jimmy McRae jumping for joy on the snowy 1979 Mintex Rally

Me in my 'office' during the 1980 Circuit of Ireland Rally

"It's still oversteering Geoff!"

Tony Pond on the 1981 Mintex Rally

Tony Pond pushes the Chevette to the limit on the 1981 Manx Rally

Tony Pond - awesome on the 1981 Manx night section
on the way to our victory

1981 Scottish Rally - happy winners!

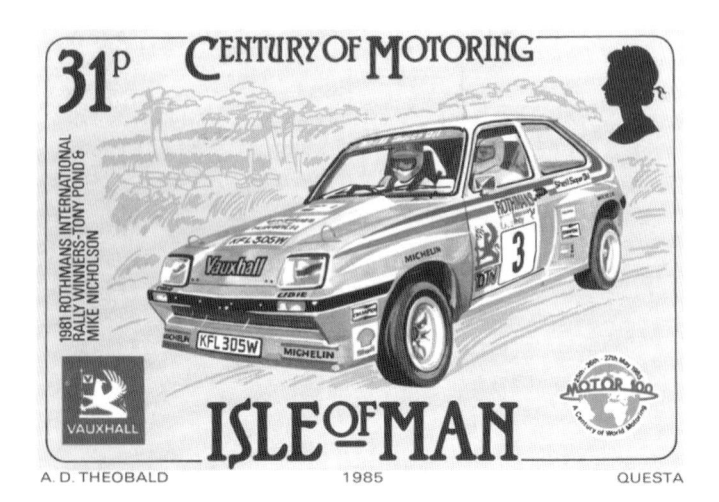

Terry Kaby 1983 - what's broken this time?

The Scottish rocks! Terry Kaby in 1983

With Terry Kaby at speed on the 1983 Manx Rally

It's not looking good! Head gasket failure on 1984 Circuit of Ireland

Kicking up the dust on our way to 2nd overall on the
1984 Scottish Rally - behind Hannu Mikkola again!

Jimmy flies the Manta on the 1984 Ulster Rally

We lost an argument with a stone wall - 1984 Circuit of Ireland

Ready for the night stages on the 1984 Ulster Rally

On our way to 7th overall on the 1984 RAC Rally

1984 RAC Rally in the Yorkshire forests

Nursing a sick engine in Wales on the 1984 RAC Rally

Jimmy McRae & Mike Nicholson
1984 British Open Rally Champions

We'll take the round black ones!
1985 Circuit of Ireland Rally with Andrew Wood

Oops! - 1985 Welsh Rally with Andrew Wood

With Andrew Wood in the mighty Astra 4S

With Derek Bell on the 1987 RAC Rally

good whatsoever. We decided we were not going to be heroes on that section during the rally itself.

The main competition came from Jean Ragnotti, with his co-driver Jean-Marc Andrie, in the Renault 5 Turbo that they had used earlier in the year to win the Monte Carlo Rally. They were great guys, very affable, with the ex-stunt driver Ragnotti being full of mischief.

The rally started in front of a huge crowd in the centre of Martigny. At the start of one of the morning stages, Jean-Marc and I walked up to the control to await our arrival time and I sat on the marshal's deck chair. Ragnotti was first on the road and, when called forward by his co-driver, rushed up the hill, executed a perfectly timed handbrake turn and knocked me flying off the chair. He thought it was hilarious!

On another occasion we were travelling slowly through a village where the French team were servicing the Renault. A fair sized crowd had gathered and, as we approached, Ragnotti rushed through the crowd and flung himself prostrate onto the road in front of us. A startled McRae only just stopped in time. One crazy, crazy man!

The huge battle continued between the two cars – it was nip and tuck all the way. The event was beautifully organised, as you might expect from the Swiss, and we were thoroughly enjoying the rally.

We approached the infamous triple caution, with the horrendous drop, rather too slowly and lost some time to the obviously braver men in the Renault. It was now beginning to look as though we were destined to finish second, with Ragnotti just edging ahead. However, as we passed through a village on a road section, Jean-Marc ran into the road and waved us down. He explained that they had a serious gearbox malfunction and would have to complete the few remaining stages slowly, so we should take no risks as we were now destined to win.

Jim and I looked at each other. Could this be right? Was the Renault really in desperate straits, or was this French gamesmanship? If true, it was a very sporting gesture by the Renault crew. We decided to push hard on the next stage, look at their time and gauge if they were telling the truth or feeding us rubbish. Sure enough, we took forty seconds out of them, so we were able to relax a little and cruise over the last three stages to a hard fought win. It was an impressive drive from Jim in the Ascona – the car was superbly planted, powerful and seemed to have no vices whatsoever.

We returned to Martigny, scrubbed up in our rented chalet and proceeded to the prize-giving. This was a typical foreign awards ceremony, held in a theatre in the middle of the town. It was full of about four hundred people and all the local dignitaries turned up. The Mayor, the Chief of Police, the Chief Fire Officer and the Rally's Clerk of the Course all gave short speeches in French, little of which we could understand, apart from when they turned to us, spoke our names, and smiled.

Then one chap stood up and in a heavy French accent read hesitantly from a piece of paper:

"We.....would like......to thank.....Jimmy and Mike......for coming all the way to Switzerland and.......taking part in our rally......."

It was pretty obvious he was far from fluent in English. Nevertheless, it was a nice gesture so I turned to the Chairman of the Rally Organisers, a jolly fellow named Pierre Schwend (he was a stout chap with a huge Jimmy Edwards style moustache and who spoke fluent English):

"Pierre," I said, "that was a really nice gesture. If I write something in English, will you translate it into French for me so that I can respond?"

"Why, of course," he replied and proceeded to write down my words in French. I walked to the microphone and began:

"Mesdames, Messieurs, les autres pilotes, les chronometreurs....c'est un rallye fantastique....."

I continued under the assumption that I was thanking everyone for organising a fabulous event and also thanking the marshals and time keepers for doing a great job. The audience listened in silence but once I had finished they stamped their feet, clapped their hands furiously and roared with laughter. I was confused - why were they laughing? John Horton, our team co-ordinator for the event and who understood some French, took me to one side and explained: "Basically translated, what you actually said was, the latch has fallen off the bog-house door and can anyone change this three-penny bit for a tap washer!"

I found out, too late, that Pierre Schwend had a reputation for being one of Switzerland's biggest practical-jokers!

We returned to our chalet having had rather too much of the free wine provided by the event's sponsor and retired to bed. One of our mechanics, Alex Strathdee, who hailed from Scotland, was particularly 'merry'! I was sharing a twin room with Jimmy who, it turned out, was a heavy snorer after drinking alcohol. I whacked him a few times with a pillow but the relief only lasted thirty seconds before the snoring started again. Alex was in a bedroom across the corridor and the noise was keeping him awake too. After shouting much abuse Alex finally 'lost it'! There was a loud metallic noise as a 'Baby Burco' came crashing through the door and into our bedroom. Jim woke momentarily, then went straight back to sleep and continued snoring. It was hilarious!

The next day's edition of the newspaper 'La Suisse' carried a fantastic front page picture of us standing on the bonnet of the Ascona on the finish ramp, spraying the champagne. As we passed through Geneva Airport's passport control for our flight home, one of the immigration guys started calling to us. He held up a copy of 'La Suisse' and, pointing to the picture on the front page, shouted: "Hey, McRae, vainqueur, vainqueur!"

Jim was puzzled. "Why are these bastards calling me a wanker?" he demanded. I didn't bother to reply!

It had been good to sit alongside Jimmy again, especially since we had just won a very different but, nevertheless, fantastic international rally.

WAL'ER WAWL!

It was back to the Chevette in September and Tony and I were fairly confident about the forthcoming Manx Rally. We had been pretty dominant on the tarmac roads of the Circuit of Ireland before our retirement and he had subsequently nicknamed the Chevette 'my silver roller-skate'. He simply loved driving the car. Nevertheless, we were not going to be complacent. The entry list included some serious competition, including a one-off entry for World Champion Walter Rohrl, in a Porsche 911, so we flew to the island early for a solid two week recce. This may sound glamorous to the uninitiated but such an undertaking is far from it. Pounding around the same familiar roads on a small island day after day, night after night, becomes a totally boring, mind-numbing nightmare.

"Not again!" I complained one evening as Tony suggested we check the notes a further time. We had already covered every stage at least a dozen times and I was at saturation point. "Listen," he said, "you will appreciate all this effort when we win the rally."

He was right, of course, so without further complaint we set off on yet another run round the island's stages.

The organisers were receiving a lot of complaints about competitors practising too quickly at night, with many exceeding the strict 50mph limit. A bulletin went out announcing that 'Judges of Fact' were to be equipped with radar speed-guns and any serious offender would be excluded from the rally. One of the worst offenders was Pentti and we thought we would relieve some of the boredom by having a bit of fun at his expense. We reversed into a farm road on the Andreas stage and waited. Sure enough, it was not long before we heard his recce car approaching at speed and, as he passed us, we put the headlights on to illuminate his car. He hit the brakes and crawled down the road convinced he had been caught! It would probably make no difference to his performance on the event, but it was good to disrupt his practice!

Walter Rohrl turned out to be a great guy and, with him being German, we couldn't resist teasing him about the war! One day, while we were checking our notes, we spotted his recce car driving slowly along the stage towards us. We stopped and quickly swapped seats. Tony opened the sunroof and stood on the passenger's seat wearing his intercom headphones. As Rohrl approached, Pond stood to attention and raised his arm in a Nazi tank commander salute, his pronounced moustache adding to the realism. Rohrl was not very amused initially but, when we stopped to have a chat, he did seem to share in the joke..........I think!

The rally itself was pretty intense. On the first stage we were surprised to find that the Chevette was not handling well. The shock absorbers were far too stiff and the car was bouncing badly over the bumps. With the competition we were facing we couldn't back off, so we had to live with the problem until the first service. We very nearly didn't get that far!

On a long, narrow and very bumpy straight section, running between two high banks, we hit a bump at high speed. The badly handling Chevette leapt into the air, hitting the following bump on its apex and launching itself again into orbit! It eventually came down, hit the road and spun a full 360 degrees........twice! The car stopped without touching anything! The road was so narrow that there could only have been a foot or so to spare at either end of the car as we spun. It was a miraculous escape but at least the car had ended up pointing in the right direction. The hot engine took a while to fire up and we set off again, having lost around a minute. It had been a very close call. At the first service area, Tony was talking about the spin to the BHP television cameras:

"We hit some bumps and spun twice," he explained, "but we didn't hit a thing. Skill that was............I had my eyes closed the whole time!"

We finished the first day lying in third position. Rohrl's Porsche was leading, with McRae's Opel second. Pentti Airikkala had retired on the second stage after a wild 'wall of death' act, followed by a roll! This was a bit of a setback for us because with Airikkala out of the rally it ensured Jimmy had won the British Championship - nobody could now catch his points total. This released him to have a real go at winning the rally, with no risk of losing his new British title.

I was chatting to Jimmy's co-driver, Ian Grindrod, at one of the service areas, when we were approached by Barrie Hinchliffe and the BHP television crew, filming the event for the BBC:

"How is it out there?" he asked, the camera rolling.

"Faster than ever," I replied. "Every year the speeds go up."

"Why is that?" he quizzed.

"Well, it's mainly due to tyre and suspension development," I answered, "plus increased engine performance and because the drivers have lost a bit more of their brain power."

".....and they didn't have that much in the first place!" quipped Grindrod. We all laughed.

"So, where will it all end?" asked Hinchliffe. Grindrod thought for a second then replied:

"It'll end with all the drivers going on their own, 'cos nobody will sit with them!" Brilliant!

We had a few hours break before the 22.30 restart for the night-time section. I had noticed before that, if Tony was ever a bit wound up, a nerve in his cheek would start twitching. He came down from his room and we sat waiting to go to the restart. I noticed that the tell-tale nerve was twitching in overdrive!

"Are you OK?" I enquired.

"Yeah," came the reply, "but I'm warning you, you're going to go round this f**kin' island like you've never gone round this f**kin' island before!" Now my own nerves started to twitch!

One of our mechanics, Ricky Bell, a large chap from Essex with a well-formed 'builders crack' on show most of the time, wandered over and was anxious to know what we were going to do to get back up the leaderboard. In particular, he wanted to know how we were going to deal with the World Champion's Porsche.

"What you gonna do about Wal'er Wawl?" he asked in his strong Essex accent.

"What do you mean Wal'er Wawl?" asked Pond.

"Wal'er Wawl," he said, "what you gonna do about Wal'er Wawl?"

"Don't know what you're talking about," insisted Pond.

"WAL'ER WAWL," our Essex man bellowed..... "WHAT YOU GONNA DO ABOUT WAL'ER WAWL?"

"What are you on about," asked Pond, "wall to wall carpets or what?"

Our confused mechanic walked away none the wiser!

We arrived at the start of the first night stage. It began in the village of Onchan before tackling the classic Injebreck section, a blindingly fast series of very high speed corners over several miles, with many crests and closely bordered by high banks and very stout trees! We set off into the night. It was nothing short of incredible, with Tony setting a devastating pace. The car was right on the ragged edge, the slick racing tyres shuddering as they fought for grip over the crests and through the following corners. I don't think I had ever been witness to such fantastic driving before or since. I had a hell of a job keeping up with the pace notes on the twisty sections. We finished safely and with me out of breath!

Rohrl had completed the stage in 12m 20s, McRae in 12m 7s – our time was an incredible 11m 47s!

"Bloody hell, Tony," I said. "You're not going to drive them all like that are you?"

"Yeah," he replied, "you'd better get used to it!"

Within three stages we were back in the lead! Without doubt Tony had been right about our comprehensive recce. All the hard work paid off, especially on the night stages. The rally was not yet finished, however, and there was still a long way to go.

It was daylight again for the last section of the rally and Rohrl and McRae were determined to wrest the lead from us. We had to keep the pressure on – if we had given either of them the merest hint that they could catch us, they would have re-doubled their efforts. We continued pretty well flat out for the rest of the rally. McRae was pushing ever harder and reduced the gap to under a minute.

We began to imagine all sorts of unusual noises coming from the car. It was running perfectly but every new rattle or 'different' sound was checked over thoroughly by the mechanics. Starting the final stage, our lead over McRae's Opel was a mere thirty-seven seconds. Unfortunately for Rohrl, the Porsche broke a drive shaft just two miles from the end, forcing the World Champion's retirement from a well deserved third place. We 'stroked' the car through the last few miles, being as gentle as we could and anxious not to lose concentration. One spin would have handed the lead to Jim. Luckily, the car and crew held together and we were relieved to return to the finish ramp on the Douglas sea-front having won the rally.

McRae was pleased too, his second overall ensuring him the British Championship, with a total of 53 points. It was a deserved win for the Scot after a fast and consistent year. Tony and I were second in the Championship, with 40 points, our two early season retirements ending any realistic chance we had of winning the overall title.

We gathered at the Villiers Hotel Rally HQ for the press conference. I'm afraid we both 'partook' of far too much alcohol and sometime later staggered out into the street looking for a lift back to our hotel. We climbed unsteadily onto one of the promenade's famous horse-drawn trams but, when we reached our destination at the far end of the bay, we realised neither of us had any money for the fare! The driver was having none of it, not being at all impressed by our 'celebrity' status and pleas for a 'freebee'. We were still in our racing overalls but he was not going to let us go without paying and an argument started. Eventually a passing rally enthusiast realised our predicament and paid the fare for us. We tottered back to our rooms to sober up in time for the awards presentation, which was being hosted by David Vine.

What a rally it had been - hard work and nerve jangling all the way! Tony's fantastic driving during the night stages lives with me to this day. After the event we were rather pleased to find that our winning Chevette was featured in a limited-edition set of Isle of Man postage stamps celebrating a Century of Motoring. We were pictured on their 31p stamp! I still have a signed first edition to this day.

WHAT WAS THAT ALL ABOUT?

In November we journeyed north to Chester for the start of the RAC Rally. The previous week had seen a hurried rebuild of our Chevette which had been badly bent at a filming session.

The BBC decided that they would follow our participation closely, with regular reports on our progress throughout the event. We took the car down to the Forest of Dean, where cameras were fitted to film on-board footage, as part of the preview. There was a thirty minute delay midway through the session while a minor problem was fixed on the car. The remote cameraman, who was filming the runs from the side of the stage, thought that the day was finished and set off back to the start, running against the stage in his Granada Estate. Unfortunately, this coincided with Tony setting off on another run! They met mid-stage on a narrow, fast corner. With nowhere to go the two cars hit head-on causing serious damage to the Chevette. The car was taken back to Blydenstein's Shepreth base where, after burning the midnight oil, it was repaired and made ready for the rally. The accident was, of course, never shown on the BBC reports!

We were quietly confident. Pond was in excellent form and the 'silver roller-skate' had proved that it was extremely competitive in the forests. Hannu Mikkola introduced the new Audi Quattro, a large and heavy four-wheel drive car which was not expected to do particularly well! We were fastest on the first stage, showing our intent for the rest of the rally. However, it was not long before we all realised that we had totally underestimated the performance of the Quattro. Mikkola simply left us all for dead, powering into a commanding lead early on, with the rest of us hanging on as best we could.

It happened that the rally coincided with both of our birthdays - mine on the 22nd November and Tony's, one day later, on the 23rd. This became fairly widespread knowledge as we travelled around the event and everywhere we went people were handing us birthday cards. It was a really nice touch. However, delivering a card was not enough for one rather lovely young lady at the start of the Ae Forest stage. We had received our start time and the marshal announced that there were thirty seconds to go. Suddenly Tony's door was pulled open and the young lady wished him a "Happy Birthday" and demanded a birthday kiss. There was considerable laughter as the girl somehow prised his full face helmet to one side and planted a big kiss on his lips. He pushed her out just as the marshal was calling "ten seconds" and we tottered off down the stage, Tony taking some time to regain his composure!

"Tony, what the hell was that all about?" I asked at the end of the stage. "How on earth did she manage to kiss you with a full face helmet on?"

"Cor," he said, "she had a tongue like a lizard!" Strangely it never seemed to happen to the co-driver even though it was his birthday too!

We were holding a strong second place but Hannu was rapidly powering out of sight. However, in the very foggy Grizedale stage, close to Windermere, he made a rare mistake and went off the road. Suddenly, we were leading the RAC Rally! It was big news for the hundreds of thousands of British fans spectating in the stages and we could hear them cheering from inside the car as we flew past, flat out. Ari Vatanen was now giving chase in his Escort and becoming a bit of a nuisance, eventually passing us to take the lead when we suffered a puncture.

We were disappointed to hear that Hannu's Quattro had regained the road without too big a time loss and we were realistic enough to realise it was only a matter of time before we were put firmly in our place. Sure enough, it was not long before he passed both us and Vatanen to re-take the lead.

By the time the rally reached the Yorkshire forests the Quattro had a ten minute lead! The stages were atrocious, extremely wet and muddy, and really suiting the four-wheel drive car at the head of the field. We were still lying third, just behind Vatanen, and we were determined to reclaim second place on the long stages through the Dalby Forest complex. Unfortunately, our Chevette ran into trouble. Halfway down one of the long and very fast Dalby Forest straights we lost all drive when the differential failed and we were forced to retire from the rally. It was a huge disappointment for us and the team, who had high hopes of a top three finish.

Eventually, Mikkola won by the huge margin of eleven minutes and we all recognised that it was the end of the competitive road for the two-wheel drive rally car on any serious stage rallies.

The end of the 1981 season inevitably brought discussions about drivers for the following year. Vauxhall and Blydenstein were very keen (as indeed I was) to retain the services of Tony Pond. Not only was he an outstanding rally driver but he was also a great ambassador for the company. His droll tone and wicked sense of humour were hugely popular with both the public and rally fans alike and he gave Vauxhall excellent public relations opportunities. However, there were hurdles to overcome. Tony wanted a World Rally programme, something that Vauxhall couldn't offer him, partly because of budget restrictions and partly because the Vauxhall marque is unique to the British Isles and little value would be gained from tackling the World Series.

Several scenarios were looked at, but it soon became obvious that dovetailing the British Rally Championship into a World programme was never going to work. Inevitably, the two parties went their separate ways and Pond eventually did a deal with Datsun to tackle a number of World Rally events, though not with any great success, if I remember correctly.

It was a disappointment for me, having had a great year with Tony. He invited me down to his lovely old beamed cottage in the village of Fingest, near Henley, for a farewell dinner. When I arrived he was slumped in a chair and not on great form.

"Are you OK?" I asked.

"No!" he replied. "I'm mentally and physically drained. I stay single to avoid this kind of thing!"

It appears that his rather 'complex' social life had finally caught up with him and there had just been a 'catfight' on the doorstep, as the two parties eyeballed each other! We retired to the village pub and got drunk!

It was in early 2002 that we heard the sad news that Tony had died. He was just fifty-six years old. It was a big shock to so many of us who were unaware that he'd been ill for some time. His funeral took place on the 16th February 2002. The congregation in the small church at Brightwell Baldwin was moved to tears as his coffin was carried through the church door with his crash helmet laid on top. It was a desperately sad day - he was a true rallying superstar and, no doubt, he and Pentti are up there, still arguing about their bridge incident on the '81 Scottish!

OK GERRY, MAYBE LATER!

Vauxhall Motors Fleet Sales Division was, by now, in full swing and enjoying great success. We organised a number of circuit-based track days around the country to further promote the brand and took along various race and rally cars, and their respective drivers, to give the fleet buyers some circuit action and an exciting day out of the office.

On one such event, held at Thruxton Circuit, Gerry Marshall brought his Opel Monza race car along. Gerry was having great fun sliding the big Monza around the circuit and terrifying his fleet passengers until they agreed to buy Vauxhall cars! He badgered me all day to sit in with him.

"You bloody rally boys think you know it all!" he barked. "Come and sit in here and I'll show you how it should be done."

"OK Gerry," I said, "maybe later."

The badgering continued all day and I eventually agreed, pulled on a helmet and sat beside him. I was determined not to be impressed and, as he set off on the first lap, I chatted aimlessly about how successful a day it had been, and pointed out an aircraft that was approaching Thruxton's airfield to land. Gerry became more determined to frighten me and went even faster. By the fourth lap he was driving way over the limit and the Monza hit the (since removed) famous bump, halfway round the ultra-fast Church Corner, at around 120mph. The car drifted wide onto the grass and became more and more sideways. Eventually we regained the track, only to spear straight across it onto the grass infield where another lurid slide followed. We found the track for a second time and Gerry slowly headed for the pits.

"Ah, I see now why you are so quick around here Gerry," I said calmly as I got out, "your line around Church is totally different to mine!"

I left him breathing heavily in the car and nonchalantly wandered off down the pit-lane. It had, of course, been a hugely impressive few laps but there was no way I was going to let him know that!

GM DEALER SPORT

During 1981 all Opel and Vauxhall dealers, operating throughout the UK, were called to a meeting at the NEC, where they were told that the two franchises were to merge and a new GM dealer network would be created to sell both marques from their showrooms. Unfortunately, this consolidation left some dealers geographically too close to each other and several were forced to close their business or change franchise.

As a result, Dealer Team Vauxhall was rebranded GM Dealer Sport. Prior to 1982, DTV management was overseen from Vauxhall's HQ in Luton, where Roy Cooke was the Motorsport Manager. Roy was also a top-class engineer who had a big input into the development of the Chevette HS and HSR. However, with the franchise re-organisation and the fact that the whole motorsport operation was still largely funded by a levy on the dealers, a committee of senior dealer principals was created to oversee the new set-up. Blydenstein Racing was still charged with running the rally team and the search for new drivers began in earnest.

Russell Brookes headed the list of candidates. He was experienced, ultra quick, and had been campaigning a Sunbeam Talbot Lotus with considerable success over the previous couple of years. However, the Talbot had let him down on a number of occasions and he seemed keen to move on. Russell would, of course, bring his long term sponsor, Andrews Heat for Hire, with him which would ease some of GM Dealer Sport's budget shortfall. It was planned to run a two car Chevette HSR campaign and this major sponsor would help fund the additional car. The deal was done and Russell, with his regular co-driver Mike Broad, joined the team.

TERRY KABY

There was still a driver vacancy for the proposed second car and eventually agreement was made with Terry Kaby to fill the seat and I was asked to co-drive for him; an invitation I readily accepted.

'TK' was a lovely chap, hailing from Towcester, and I was delighted to be joining him. He had seen considerable success over previous years in various Minis, Datsun Violets and, latterly, the awesome TR7 V8 and would be a valuable addition to the team.

The 1982 Mintex Rally was the first outing for the new Kaby/Nicholson pairing. The British Rally Championship was still hugely popular and once again the entry list was filled with familiar names: Mikkola, Airikkala, Vatanen, Toivonen, Eklund and Blomqvist were all there, as well as the usual top drivers from the UK. We would be facing some very stiff competition.

As expected, Mikkola remained untouchable during the event and simply powered away from the rest of us, though behind him there were some good scraps among the two-wheel drive brigade. 'TK' settled into the Chevette very quickly. We had a good battle with McRae and Brookes and, by mid-event, we were leading the Brit-pack in fourth place overall, just behind World Champion Ari Vatanen and Airikkala, who were second and third. Eventually, we finished a pleasing fifth overall, behind McRae and just ahead of team-mate Brookes. It was a good start to our campaign and things were looking positive.

The Circuit of Ireland was a different story though. Terry was confident in the car on tarmac and we were absolutely flying. We were holding down a fine third overall as the rally journeyed south into the Republic, but sadly it was not to last. We were nearing the end of a long stage, on a very fast section, when the Chevette hit a patch of unseen gravel and spun violently. We hit the bank, tearing off the front suspension in the process, and rolled! It had all happened so quickly. We couldn't understand why, on a stage that had been completely free of gravel up to that point, there was a large patch, hidden from view, just over a crest. The answer came a little later.

After the service crew retrieved the car we decided to spectate and walked about half a mile into a stage to watch the action just before the first corner. Shortly afterwards a bunch of Irish lads arrived, several carrying small sacks over their shoulders. They carefully selected a suitable place and emptied the contents of the bags onto the road! It was gravel, and it explained everything! We had a go at them, relating how similar antics had caused us to crash, but they were not in a mood to listen. The first car on the road was Henri Toivonen, who arrived at high speed. We waved him down - he slowed and survived the corner. By now we were in danger of being lynched so we returned to the stage start to warn the other drivers of the man-made hazard. I was pretty hacked off that we should fall foul of such idiots and reported the incidents to the Clerk of the Course but, to be honest, he wasn't very surprised.

Happily for Vauxhall, Russell and Mike Broad finished second overall behind McRae's Opel, with Toivonen third. Toivonen's effort was particularly heroic as he was driving with an injured and heavily bandaged hand following an earlier 'off' on day one.

The Welsh International would not, sadly, see our fortunes change. The entry list saw all the usual protagonists with the exception of Hannu Mikkola, who was elsewhere on World Rally duties. His place was taken by Bjorn Waldegard, which left a glimmer of hope for the two-wheel drive brigade, the amiable Swede being totally unfamiliar with the big Quattro. However, we were all to be disappointed when he took an immediate lead and was never headed, eventually winning by over two minutes from Toivonen. Jim McRae and Ian Grindrod were sidelined on Epynt when they had a huge accident, wrecking the Opel but luckily causing them no personal damage. We ran strongly for the first half of the rally before stopping with transmission failure and suffering another disappointing retirement from a good position.

Work-wise, Vauxhall's new Fleet Team was going great guns. For too many years Ford had dominated the scene and many large company fleet personnel were tired of their 'take it or leave it' approach. They were ready for a change and we were delighted to offer it, with the new set up at Vauxhall determined to give excellent customer service. Company after company switched allegiance and our market share improved dramatically, with Ford's share going the other way! The factory at Luton was in full flow churning out the additional demand and Vauxhall became the 'blue-eyed boys' of GM Europe.

I was asked to take over as Regional Fleet Manager for the Greater London area, where many of the UK's largest corporations were based. Unfortunately, this meant a move from Yorkshire as I needed to be based closer to Vauxhall's Luton Headquarters, so we moved to Leighton Buzzard in Bedfordshire.

Terry and I were desperately hoping for a better result on the Scottish Rally having failed to finish the previous two events through no real fault of our own. Mikkola was back in his Quattro but, for once, his luck deserted him. On the first stage, his steering broke and he was forced to reverse the car to the end, losing over six minutes as a result.

Everyone else perked up – perhaps it would be someone else's turn to win!

A rally-long battle ensued between the Escorts, the Asconas and our two Chevettes. Places swapped continually as the odd puncture or minor 'off' changed fortunes. We were all so engrossed in the fight that none of us noticed the fast recovering Mikkola, as the Quattro climbed back up the leaderboard. He passed us, then Brookes, then Toivonen and then Malcolm Wilson in quick fashion. He was, however, running out of time to pass the rally leader McRae, with the Scot wringing every ounce of performance from the Opel to stay in front. It was, of course, to no avail and inevitably the Audi and its dominant crew arrived at the finish in first place, with McRae as the bridesmaid on his home event. "You can call me McSecond McRae!" he complained.

We finished a pleasing sixth but, like the rest of the field, we were pretty fed up with being so soundly beaten by the four-wheel drive Audi.

The Manx was next and we spent considerable time on the island refining our pace notes. It was a tough event with 46 stages and 380 stage miles, over three full days. Terry was well up for it though and, by the end of day one, we were lying second overall, just behind Toivonen's Opel Ascona 400. We were slowed a little on day two with a persistent misfire and dropped to fourth place.

Sadly, though, the engine finally cried enough and expired - another retirement and another disappointment.

Having retired from the event we decided to go and spectate. There was a rumour going around the island that Ari Vatanen was bound to have a 'big one'. He was driving a plain black Ford Escort that was exceptionally quick but suffering from terrible handling. We saw it on a bumpy straight and we, too, came to the same conclusion - he couldn't go on like that and survive the full event! The car's set up was all over the place - it was careering from side to side on any undulations and was obviously a real handful.

Eventually 'it came to pass' that Mr. Vatanen 'partook' of the big accident! Terry Harryman, his Northern Ireland born co-driver, was no spring chicken and enjoyed many a fag but, even by his standards, he looked positively ill as the rally wore on, and was chain smoking in the service areas.

They hit a bump on the Staarvey stage and the twitchy car finally got away from the 'Flying-Finn', rolling several times and eventually coming to rest upside down in the ditch outside a small cottage, badly damaged. They crawled out of the wreckage and, according to spectators, Harryman turned to Ari and enquired in his Irish accent:

"Ari, is the car droivable?"

"No, no, no!" said Vatanen. "For sure you can see, it cannot move."

"Oh, thank Christ for that!" retorted the very relieved co-driver, and lit up another fag!

It was a day of carnage. First, Mikkola's Quattro retired. It had been well off the pace throughout the event, with both engine and transmission problems. Then, Henri Toivonen missed a fast right-hand bend in fog and crashed, handing the lead to Jimmy McRae's Opel Ascona and this, in turn, elevated our team-mates Brookes and Broad to second overall, so Vauxhall managed one decent result at least.

We entered the Lombard RAC Rally, but inevitably retired from a strong top ten placing on stage fifty-five with a broken rear axle. 1982 had not been a good year and really held no good memories for me, though it had been fun rallying with Terry. He was a top bloke.

Terry had shown a lot of pace between the various mechanical failures we'd suffered during 1982 and the team was pleased to keep him on for another year with me in the co-driver's seat again.

The two of us had been concerned about the reliability of our Chevette during the previous year. While Russell's car behaved impeccably, ours had often succumbed to engine and transmission failures. Kaby was not particularly hard on the car and drove with mechanical sympathy, so it was not down to driving style nor, I believed, just bad luck.

It had all been rather familiar to me. During my first year with Jimmy McRae, in 1979, we had been suspicious that some of the parts we were using were, shall we say, a little 'long in the tooth' and perhaps beyond their sell-by date, saving budget in order to maintain Airikkala's car in tip-top condition. It was just a feeling that we had at the time, and Terry and I were pretty sure that we had suffered in a similar manner!

Whatever, we were hoping for better reliability in 1983, but it wasn't to be. In fact it would go down as the worst year of my rallying career. The

Chevette was competitive enough and we were often lying in good positions, but the results just didn't come, usually due to mechanical failure.

On the Mintex we held fifth overall for most of the rally, an event that will go down in history as having some of the worst conditions ever encountered in the Yorkshire forests. Deep snow, ice and thick fog made it very difficult for the crews. It looked as if we would be heading for a reasonable result lying just behind our team-mates Brookes and Broad. However, a puncture caused us to spin into a deep ditch, costing us many minutes. We finally finished the rally in a lowly fifteenth place and hugely disappointed. Brookes upheld Vauxhall honours in fourth place overall.

On the Circuit of Ireland we held third place for much of the event but mechanical trouble saw us retire. We fared no better on the Welsh where we lost six minutes due to brake failure, causing us to go off and we eventually retired with electrical issues. However, Russell Brookes was continuing his good run, finishing a fine second overall behind the Quattro of Stig Blomqvist, albeit over eight minutes behind. The Audi was still blowing away the opposition, covering the stages two seconds a mile faster than any of the two-wheel drive cars – which was ridiculous in our view!

Surely the Scottish would treat us better? Unfortunately it was not to be - after another strong showing we retired yet again with engine problems.

What about the Ulster Rally? Nope! Lying in a strong fourth place overall, the Chevette's engine gave up the ghost within sight of the finish!

The Manx Rally? Well, Toivonen won from Ari Vatanen, and we had better reliability for once, finishing fourth overall just behind our team-mate Russell Brookes, whose Chevette was its usual paragon of reliability. It had been a great year for both himself and co-driver Mike Broad and we were made up for them.

We were convinced our reliability problems were due to insufficient budget to run two cars properly. Russell was rightly the number one driver in the team but keeping his car reliable at the head of the field came, I fear, at the expense of any real opportunity for our own success.

I was glad to see the back of the 1983 British Championship series. Now we only had the RAC Rally remaining to salvage our year. Of course you won't be surprised to know that we finished on yet another low. This time, though, it was not the fault of the car.

Once again, Terry had been driving well and we were comfortably inside the top fifteen as we arrived for the Welsh stages. It was very cold and there had been a dusting of snow, leaving the stages very, very icy. It was also a very dark night.

We set off on the long Penmachno Forest stage, just outside Betws-y-Coed. After three miles or so we negotiated a hairpin left and accelerated down a 300 yard straight. The road was not, unfortunately, shown on the OS map and, as we approached a crest at the end of the straight, we could see in the distance ahead some trees that 'obviously' marked a tee junction, so we took the crest at speed. It was a wrong move! Immediately over the crest, the road went 90 degrees right. Ahead lay a deep gorge with some spindly trees growing up its sides. The car spun on the ice and went straight off backwards at a fair old speed. We went over the edge and rolled end over end, finishing some 90 feet down the gorge, nose first in a stream. I remember that it was all totally surreal! Everything happened in slow motion, with the car's lights illuminating the banking on the inside of the corner as we spun. This was covered with many spectators and, as we disappeared over the edge, I was conscious of hundreds of flash bulbs going off together as they captured our 'moment' with their cameras!

We were both OK but obviously out of the event. We heard from some of the spectators, after we had crawled up the bank, that they had been slowing the approaching cars before our arrival but had got rather bored with seeing no action. We were the first car they had not flagged down. Cheers!

Some hours later the car was retrieved. It needed the services of two Land Rovers and a Unimog (a large utility 4x4 vehicle) chained together to pull the car up the steep ravine. The front wheels kept catching on the stumps of the trees that we had demolished, preventing the car from moving. We needed someone in the car to turn the wheel left or right, as appropriate, to avoid the stumps. One of the rescue crew volunteered, so we strapped him in the driver's seat. The car was then pulled up the steep ravine and was within a couple of feet of the road when the towing eye gave way under the weight and pulled out of the

Chevette's rear bodywork. The car plunged back down to the bottom of the ravine, the 'driver' screaming as it fell. He refused to do it a second time!

So the 1983 season ended, as did my two years with 'TK'. He had been great company but it had been a truly awful year for both of us. I was sad for Terry, the Chevette's unreliability had done little to further his career though he was, in my view, a fine driver and deserved better.

After two years of non-finishes, I'd had enough and I thought seriously about retiring. However, I decided to wait and see what turned up before I walked away.

MANTA MAGIC

At the end of 1983 Bill Blydensteins's contract with Vauxhall was terminated and a completely new motorsport organisation was put in place. GM Dealer Sport now took charge of the rally effort and their committee opened new premises in Milton Keynes, from where they prepared the cars and ran the team. John Nixey headed up the day to day operations. The 1984 Team would consist of two Opel Manta 400 Group 'B' rally cars. The new Manta, which replaced the successful Ascona 400, was some 70kgs lighter than the previous car, being a two door coupe version with lightweight panels. Power had been increased slightly to 280bhp.

Russell Brookes and Mike Broad took one car, moving over from the previously campaigned Chevette HSR, and Jimmy McRae took the second with me co-driving for him once again. I was pleased that I had made no hasty decision to retire at the end of 1983! It was a great feeling to be back with Jim, having enjoyed my time with him in the DTV Chevette and also during the Swiss Rallye du Vin, which we won in the Ascona, in 1981.

There wasn't a great deal of love lost between Russell and Jimmy. They were, I suppose, always going to have a difficult relationship, both fighting to be the British 'top dog' and neither prepared to give any quarter in order to achieve that position. On the other hand, I enjoyed a great working relationship with Mike Broad. We had known each other for many years, having been joint organisers of the Shenstone Rally in the early '70s and we always got on well.

As usual, the first round of the 1984 British Open Championship was the 'Mintex Rally', now renamed the National Breakdown Rally in deference to its new sponsor. Mikkola's Quattro was expected to be as dominant as ever, with the minor placings being fought over by the usual gaggle of two-wheel drive cars, including our two Mantas.

Fog again hit the rally and provided the crews with a very big challenge. Once again the foreign crews were complaining about 'those maps' that the UK co-drivers were using to guide their drivers through the stages; the maps were actually nothing special. We merely read the roads from the fairly accurate Ordnance Survey maps of the area – our foreign foes could have done the same but were not confident in doing so. It did give us a considerable advantage in the foggy conditions though.

In Cropton Forest, at night and still in thick fog, we suffered a front wheel puncture several miles from the end of the stage. We kept going as fast as possible with the map information helping to keep our speed up in the foggy conditions. At the stage finish we were only four seconds slower than the Quattro, as Hannu Mikkola and co-driver Arne Hertz struggled in the poor visibility. Under normal circumstances, with the puncture, we could have expected to lose the best part of a minute to him. Using the maps was again proving to be very beneficial though, in truth, they only gave an indication of what lay ahead and were far less accurate than having reliable pace notes. They also had their dangers!

At the end of the stage we jumped out and quickly changed the punctured wheel. The following stage, Pickering Forest, started just a few hundred yards down the public road and always used the same start-line, just 100 yards in from the entrance gate. It then commenced with a point eight of a mile long straight, ending in a tightening right-hander. I was busy replacing my seat belts and crash helmet and getting everything in order as we approached the stage arrival control, still in very thick fog.

I received our start time and proceeded to brief Jim on the stage characteristics:

"OK, Jim," I said, "this starts with a point eight of a mile straight, ending in an open but tightening right-hander. I'll count down the distance to the corner."

We set off down the stage, with Jim throwing caution to the wind as I used the trip-meter:

"....point six....point five.... point four......"

We could barely see a hundred yards in front of us, and at point three of a mile to the corner, and still flat out in fifth gear, I was about to tell Jim to slow for the bend. Before I could say anything we were confronted by the sight of three or four red Marlboro anoraks appearing out of the fog, their wearers running like hell! I distinctly remember their arms pumping furiously as they leapt out of harm's way. We had arrived at the corner earlier than anticipated! Jim slammed the wheel hard over but we went off the road, taking to the bank on the outside of the corner and demolishing the fence on top. He kept his foot in and we just managed to regain the road after a huge moment. We were still fastest on the stage though!

Afterwards I tried to work out what had gone wrong and, looking at the road book, it dawned on me that I had been so busy at the stage arrival getting my 'office' in order after the puncture, that I hadn't noticed, in the fog, that the stage had, for once, started some two-tenths further from the entrance than usual. This had thrown my countdown into disarray!

The 'Marlboro' spectators came to find us at the finish. Evidently the three or four cars running ahead of us on the stage had been approaching fairly cautiously and they were horrified when we arrived, still at full chat and very nearly wiping them out in the process!

No-one was surprised when, in spite of the earlier foggy conditions, Mikkola's Quattro won. Jimmy and I were second, 5m 38s behind, with

Russell Brookes a mere twenty-two seconds further behind us. It had been a good battle between the two Manta drivers - no quarter was asked and none given throughout the whole event.

The celebrations were muted however, when it was learned that the popular Icelandic driver, Hafsteinn Hauksson had been killed when his Escort collided with a tree in Wykeham Forest. Hafsteinn was one of life's true gentlemen, and his sad loss was felt by everyone.

It was soon Easter and time for the Circuit of Ireland Rally. The good news for us was the non-appearance of Hannu Mikkola, who was away on World Championship duties. Competition would still be fierce though, with the German driver, Harold Demuth, taking over the Quattro. Henri Toivonen would also, no doubt, prove to be a tough competitor in the Rothmans Porsche 911. There was an abundance of Manta 400s on the event. In addition to our two GM Dealer Sport cars were entries from the trio of top Irish drivers: Bertie Fisher, Billy Coleman and Austin McHale.

Jim and I shot into an early lead, the Manta proving to be an absolutely fantastic tarmac car. Early competition from Toivonen was curtailed when he punctured both rear tyres and lost over six minutes. Russell Brookes was the next retirement when his prop-shaft broke at high speed, wrecking the underside of the Manta and forcing him out of the rally on the spot. It was a very strange failure. No-one in the team could remember anything like it happening before and it was decided to keep a close watch on our own Manta's transmission.

However, our troubles were not to stem from the transmission. In our case we suffered engine problems when the head gasket failed towards the end of the first day. We struggled to get the car back to the final service of the day, where the mechanics set about the mammoth task of replacing the cylinder head gasket. We were running out of time, so I walked to the 'Service Out' control and waited for the car to arrive. Jim rushed to the exit of the service area at high speed and we booked in with just three seconds remaining before exclusion! The car was placed in parc ferme overnight, with more work required to finish the repair the following morning.

Nevertheless, we were still in the rally, though suffering from an engine that was 'down on power', having been subjected to several stage miles at over 110 degrees during the previous day.

We had a pretty nasty moment on a stage just south of the border. We hit a patch of gravel as we entered a right-hand corner. The car understeered off the road, punched through a stone wall and leapt into a field. I climbed out and opened a gate to enable Jim to regain the road, but the Manta, being on slick racing tyres, was having difficulty climbing the slight incline on the wet grass. Out of the corner of my eye I spotted the farmer running up the field towards us and he wasn't happy! Shouting and waving a large stick, he was intent on 'sorting us out'. It was a race against time! Would Jim reach the road before the very angry farmer arrived? It was a close call but I just managed to jump in the car as the old guy reached us, shouting obscenities. We shot off, having lost a couple of minutes or so.

The front spoiler had been totally destroyed by the impact with the wall and later on the same stage, as we flew over a crest on a long and very fast straight, we were to learn how much aerodynamic influence the spoiler had. Without its downforce, the car reared up as it took off over the crest, with its nose pointing high into the sky and becoming almost vertical! Luckily, the car regained level flight and performed a heavy but safe landing. We continued at a much slower pace to the stage finish!

Unfortunately, our participation was not to last. The cylinder head gasket failed for a second time in the middle of the fabulous Sally Gap stage and this time we were forced to retire. With both GM Dealer Sport Mantas now out of the rally, it was time to return to Belfast. The car was despatched on its trailer, while we returned with the 'chase' crews in their Carlton Estates. These three cars were all British registered and had radio aerials on the roof! Not, then, ideal transport for the run north through the 'bandit country' around the border town of Dundalk! As we approached the town's outskirts we came across a large group of people marching up the road towards us, waving banners and blocking all traffic. Being Easter Sunday we assumed it was an Easter Parade and pulled over to the side of the road ready to get out and give them a wave.

One of our passengers was a Northern Ireland Vauxhall dealer, Crawford Harkness, whose showroom was in Ballymena. He understood the score!

"Listen carefully," he said over the radio, "this is f**kin' serious. Lock the doors, look straight ahead, and do absolutely nothing!"

It was a good job that we took his advice. It was a 'No Extradition' march organised by IRA sympathisers! Several hundred marchers were watched over by a single Irish Garda walking ahead of them. It was a nerve-wracking time as they slowly threaded their way past, shouting slogans and giving our cars the odd shove. We were mightily relieved when they had finally passed and we were able to continue on our way.

There was the usual carnage on this tough Irish rally, with the entry list decimated by accidents and mechanical woes. Opel Manta honours were upheld, however, after a fine win by Billy Coleman.

Normal service was resumed for Audi on the Welsh Rally, when Hannu Mikkola powered the Quattro to an easy win from our team-mate Brookes, who came in second. Malcolm Wilson brought his private Quattro home in third place, while we finished fourth following a host of punctures.

The 1984 Scottish Rally proved to be good for us, finishing second overall behind Hannu Mikkola's Quattro which, as usual, won with ease. There was simply no way we could match the performance of the four-wheel drive machine, with its masterful Finnish driver in his usual fine form. Russell completed the podium with a good third overall.

At the end of every stage our on-board television camera caught my first words to the marshals and I always asked the same question:

"What did Hannu do?" Followed by the inevitable sigh!

I was still receiving lectures from Jim about the appalling treatment of the Scots by the English over the centuries. Very early one morning, after we had been tackling rough forest stages all night, we were on a road section and feeling pretty tired. Suddenly the intercom came alive:

"Can you see those fields over there?" asked Jim.

"Yes!" I replied.

"Can you see how green they are?"

"Yep!"

"Well, that's Bannockburn, and the fields are green because they've been fed by the blood of the English Sassenach bastards that dared to cross the border!" he bellowed.

I loved it and we roared with laughter, my Scottish history education was finally complete!

We had quite a treat on the way back into Glasgow for the finish. The Glasgow Constabulary provided the top three finishers, Mikkola's Quattro, our Manta and Ari Vatanen's Escort, with a motorcycle police escort to the finish ramp. There were six motorbikes, their riders well on top of their game. We drove for some ten miles through the outskirts of the city at high speed, desperately trying to keep up with them. At every set of traffic lights two bikes raced ahead and stopped the traffic, while we roared through regardless of whether the lights were green or red. At one point we even went down the wrong side of a dual carriageway to avoid a traffic jam! It was every bit as exciting as the rally itself!!

In the lead up to the Ulster Rally one of our neighbours had woken in the middle of the night to find someone in their bedroom. Thinking it was one of his young children, he switched the light on. He was horrified to find an intruder at the end of his bed, wearing a balaclava and holding a shotgun. Our neighbour told the guy he could take the car keys and any money that was in the house if he would leave immediately. However, it became obvious that the chap was not interested in anything other than his wife. It was a very frightening situation and he lunged at the intruder. In the melee that followed, the shotgun went off and removed two of our neighbour's fingers as the intruder fled down the stairs and made his escape.

This was not to be an isolated incident and several other similar attacks took place in and around the Leighton Buzzard area over the following four weeks. The place was crawling with police day and night but the intruder was very elusive. At night, armed police would stay in our houses, leaving downstairs windows and doors open to try and tempt the fugitive to enter, with the residents instructed to stay upstairs no matter what happened down below! Few of us could sleep with police helicopters hovering over various housing areas, their searchlights ablaze.

Eventually, the police captured the chap. One evening, an off-duty police officer heard a group of men in the local rugby club talking about the 'fox', as the fugitive had become known. This was nothing unusual for it was just about the sole topic of conversation in the local pubs and clubs. However, it became obvious to the policeman that one individual in the group was discussing details that were not in the public domain. Suspicious, he followed the chap's car as he left to return to his home, which turned out to be in North London. He called for back-up and they broke into the house. Inside they found the balaclava and the shotgun and he was immediately arrested. It was a massive relief to everyone in the Leighton Buzzard area, especially to me as his arrest came just before the Ulster Rally. I had considered stepping down from the event, not wishing to leave my family alone in such a stressful situation. I arrived in Belfast for the recce, somewhat exhausted, both mentally and physically!

During the recce we were making notes on a stage close to the border with the Republic when we had a bit of a fright. We rounded a corner to find three chaps standing in the middle of the road holding a banner which simply said 'McRAE STOP'. It was still the time of 'the troubles' in Northern Ireland and, slightly worried, we pulled up. One of the chaps leaned in the window and said in a broad Irish accent, in what we took to be a rather threatening tone: "Jimmy, me mother is your greatest fan and you will join her for a cup of tea!" It was an instruction not a request, so we both complied with the order and joined the good lady and her sons for a welcome cup of tea and a piece of cake!

With the recce over, the rally began and we arrived at the start of the first stage. We were seeded Number 2 behind Walter Rohrl who was testing a new, more powerful, Audi in the form of the Quattro Sport. This short-wheel base rally car produced no less than 420bhp from its latest engine. We sat on the start line and watched in awe as Rohrl powered the car off the start line. In a blink of an eye it was at the end of the first straight and had disappeared at eye-watering speed around the first corner! Like a lamb to the slaughter we set off. It seemed to take an age for the Manta to arrive at the first corner that the

Quattro had reached in a few seconds! The scene was set though, and Rohrl continued to dominate the event, taking an average of 2.3 seconds per stage mile out of the next fastest car.......our Manta!

We put the Audi out of our minds and enjoyed a great battle, not only with our rival and team-mate Brookes, but also with the Manta 400 of local favourite, Bertie Fisher. It was nip and tuck all the way. Fisher then rolled his car on a slippery corner, losing six minutes, and we spun in the same place, losing thirty seconds to Russell which put him just ahead of us.

I was not on my usual form, the fatigue caused by the recent 'fox' activities at home somewhat affecting my performance. I lost my place in the notes a couple of times, which was not like me at all, and I was generally not on top of my game. It wasn't affecting our speed though!

On one moorland stage we were flat out on a long straight, and travelling at well over 100mph, when the car hit a bump which we had failed to notice during our slow-speed recce. The Manta suffered from rather short rear suspension travel and the axle hit the bump-stops, kicking the rear of the car high into the air. The car bumped along the road, literally on its nose, still at very high speed. It finally came back down with a 'crash' and went into a major 'tank slapper'!

It was a very nasty moment and my throat constricted with the stress of it all, my voice rising at least three octaves as I gathered myself together and continued reading the notes! We reached the end of the stage without further incident and I handed the time cards to the marshal. I turned and looked at Jim, our eyes met, and he just said quietly: "F**kin' hell!" It summed it up perfectly!

Russell stayed just ahead of us throughout the rest of the rally as we traded times, stage after stage. We eventually arrived at the start of the final stage having clawed ourselves back to just three seconds behind our team-mate's Manta. It was game on! This last stage was very wet, however, and we hit a patch of standing water just before a junction, promptly locking up and overshooting the turn, losing fifteen seconds and handing second place to Brookes in the process, and confirming our third place. Walter Rohrl won by a country mile, of course - it was just another nail in the coffin for the two-wheel drive brigade!

In September we crossed the Irish Sea to the Isle of Man. The Manx Rally would decide the winner of the 1984 Open Championship, the fight being between ourselves and our team-mates Russell Brookes and co-driver Mike Broad. It was going to be a tough event. As ever, the entry list contained some of the best rally drivers from around the world. Juha Kankunnen drove the Rothmans backed Porsche for the first time in the UK and, of course, Mikkola was out again in the Quattro.

Tony Pond was entered in a Group A version of the Rover 3500, a very large car to squeeze through the narrow Manx lanes. The big Rover was hampered by the Group A technical regulations, its gearbox being lumbered with a very high first gear. This was affecting the car's ability to accelerate away from stage starts and tight hairpin bends, the sticky rear racing tyres refusing to break grip and 'bogging' the engine down.

The Leyland mechanics came up with an ingenious solution, quite literally! They mounted a small tank in the rear of the car and filled it with a 50/50 mixture of Fairy Liquid and water, with pipes leading from the tank to the rear tyres. When wheel spin was required to overcome the high first gear, co-driver Rob Arthur simply flicked a switch and sprayed the soapy solution onto the rear tyres, causing them to break traction. This also had the side effect of creating a great deal of tyre smoke which was heartily applauded by the appreciative spectators!

Brookes powered off to a quick start on the foggy opening stages, with us close behind. Kankunnen retired the Porsche with no oil pressure and a blown engine on stage four, while Mikkola's gearbox broke on the same stage, putting both cars out on the spot. Hallelujah, there is a God! Russell punctured and we found ourselves leading the rally by two minutes at the start of day two. Then we also punctured and lost our two minute advantage. We were now neck and neck with the Andrews Heat for Hire Manta, with us just a few precious seconds ahead.

There followed a no-holds-barred fight between the two GM Dealer Sport Mantas - it was very close, each of us taking turns to be fastest. The management were getting very twitchy! Gradually, though, Russell seemed to be getting the upper hand and was slowly closing on us for the lead.

Tackling the Tholt-y-Will stage, we were absolutely flat out and right on the ragged edge responding to Russell having just taken two seconds out of us on the previous Andreas stage. On the approach to the actual Hill Climb, just before the hairpins, there was a very fast section leading to a tight left and right over a narrow bridge. It was damp under the trees and, in the braking area, we only just slowed enough to turn into the left-hander and cross over the bridge. The Manta 'wet tarmac understeer' raised its ugly head and we just, and I mean only just, missed the bridge parapet.

We continued to the end of the stage and waited for Brookes, who was running behind us, to check his time.

"If he's beaten us on that one," said Jim, "it's over, I cannae go any faster!" I agreed with him!
We waited and waited and, after two or three minutes, Jim said: "OK, let's go, I know where he is!"

Sure enough, Russell had destroyed his Manta after hitting the same bridge parapet and wiping off his front suspension.

That gave us a twelve minute lead, with most of the serious competition having crashed or retired, and with still a day and a half to go! Complacency set in and concentration went out of the window! Jim misheard the note "turn ninety left" at a junction and, braking too late, locked up and ploughed through some tape, nearly hitting a dozen or so spectators. Later, I managed to turn over two pages at once in the pace notes. As far as I was concerned the notes still reflected the road perfectly! They seemed to be working fine to me, until I heard Jim's question over the intercom:

"What the f**k are you talking about?" he asked.

Luckily, we survived our lapses to take an easy win and along with it the British Open Rally Championship.

I was elated. It had been a long and hard fight for the title, against massive opposition from many quarters, not least from our team-mates Brookes and Broad. The Manta had been supremely reliable, with the exception of the Circuit of Ireland engine problem. It was a superb rally car and we both loved it.

Bertie Fisher brought his Manta 400 home in a deserved second place, and Tony Pond survived late rear axle problems to finish an excellent third in the big Rover.

There were a few high jinks after the rally. We were staying in the Palace Hotel overlooking the seafront on the Douglas promenade. It was quite a modern hotel by Isle of Man standards, and the bathrooms had toilet handles fitted flush to the wall, with the cisterns being hidden from view! These cisterns could be accessed for service or repair through wooden panels on the corridor walls. We knew Jim was taking a bath so we unscrewed the access panel, reached in and flushed the toilet. Jim stopped singing and lay quietly, wondering what had happened. A couple of minutes later we did it again, and then a third time, leaving my driver very confused. He had once owned a plumbing business but had never come across automatic toilet flushing before!

Russell often insisted he was a bit of a wine buff and always ordered expensive bottles of wine at the dinner table, spouting on about what a "good year 1979 had been", and so on. The rest of us usually ordered the house wine. On one particular evening he was called away from the dinner table to take a phone call so we grabbed an empty wine bottle from the next table and poured Russell's expensive wine into it. We filled his now empty bottle with our cheap wine. When he returned we studied him carefully as he carried on drinking 'his' wine, but he never noticed any difference! He didn't even raise an eyebrow! We never let on....until now!

The Palace Hotel was really not worth its four stars, though its staff considered it to be the best on the island and consequently tended to be a bit 'up themselves'. One evening the Head Waiter asked Russell for his dinner order.

"I'd like egg and chips please," said Russell.

"We don't *do* egg and chips, Sir," replied the rather haughty waiter.

"Hang on," said Russell, "on the menu you've got pommes-frites with the fillet steak, haven't you?"

"Yes Sir, but we don't *do* eggs with them!"

"And here, you've got gammon with egg or pineapple," continued Russell undaunted.

"Correct Sir, but we don't *do* egg and chips."

"I'll tell you what then," insisted Russell, "I'll have the chips off the steak dish and the egg off the gammon dish!"

The waiter disappeared in a huff. A short time later he pushed a trolley to the table, on top of which sat a large silver salver. He and two other waiters stood around the trolley, paused, and then ceremoniously opened the lid to reveal.........a large plate of egg and chips! We all applauded and the hotel charged Russell for two meals, which he gladly paid!

The GM Dealer Sport Committee was always looking for additional sponsorship and they approached the builders, Wimpey Homes, to see if any interest could be raised. Wimpey seemed quite open to the idea and it was arranged that Jimmy and the Championship winning Manta 400 would be entered as a course car on a Welsh forest rally that was to start in Llandrindod Wells during October. Members of the Wimpey Board agreed to come along and sit in the co-driver's seat during the event to give them some idea of what rallying was all about, allowing them to evaluate any marketing opportunities from the proposed association.

The Wimpey helicopter duly landed on a local school playing field and deposited their Managing

Director, accompanied by two other senior directors, who would share the co-driving between them during the day. They had arranged for a photographer to record the day's activities and he was also charged with taking aerial shots of the rally car in the forests. I sat in the co-pilot's seat to navigate the helicopter and follow the action. Our pilot was ex-army and had only recently returned from the Falklands conflict and was not averse to having a bit of fun. We had a great time following the Manta through the stages, a couple of hundred feet above the trees, with me reading the road from 'those maps' to the pilot in good rally fashion! Our aviator was throwing the aircraft all over the place – it was tremendous fun!

The Wimpey Directors enjoyed themselves but, unfortunately, were unable to see any real opportunities for them in future sponsorship of the team. It was a great day out though!

The 1984 RAC Rally started from Chester and consisted of 56 special stages through the Lake District, Scotland, and the Kielder and North Yorkshire forests, before completing a loop around Wales. As ever, it would prove to be a tough event, with all the top World Championship protagonists out on the rally. Ari Vatanen arrived with the new Peugeot 205 T16, an ultra-competitive four-wheel drive car, and Audi were represented by three Quattros in the hands of Mikkola, Blomqvist and Michelle Mouton.

Ignoring them as they all powered away from the rest of the field, a massive battle ensued between the leading British drivers for the 'two-wheel drive' rally. Jim and I enjoyed a trouble free run and everything was going well until we reached Wales on the last leg of the event. Then, unfortunately, we suffered another head gasket failure, and the Manta ran with an extremely hot engine for many stage miles before it could be replaced. Having finally cured the problem we were running strongly again when an under-bonnet oil pipe split, spraying thick lubricant onto the windscreen. This had happened to us once before during the 1980 Manx Rally in the Chevette! We had to stop several times mid-stage to clean the oil off the screen – it was night-time and the lubricant completely obliterated our view ahead. Our engine never really recovered from its earlier overheating and began to sound really sick so we decided to back off and nurse the car through the rest of the event.

Vatanen won, the Peugeot beating the previously all-conquering Quattros, with Mikkola being the 'bridesmaid' for once! We eventually finished seventh overall, with team-mate Russell finishing a fine fifth to cap a good year for the GM Dealer Sport team.

I had now been rallying in various works teams for over ten years and, having achieved the British Rally Championship win, I was again thinking seriously about hanging my helmet up for good. The GMDS Committee understood my position and I prepared to walk away from rallying to continue my career with Vauxhall Motors.

ANDREW WOOD

A short while later, I was telephoned by John Nixey, the GM Dealer Sport competitions boss, who told me that they had been closely watching a young Scottish rally driver, Andrew Wood. He had been putting in some very competitive drives and it was thought he would make a good addition to the team, driving the Group A Astra GTE which was proposed for the following year's Open Championship, to run alongside the Mantas. It was felt that a co-driver of my experience would help to bring him along at a sensible pace. It would certainly be a new challenge and I gave it serious thought, eventually agreeing to do the job and putting my retirement on hold yet again.

I joined forces with Andrew in the Astra GTE in time for the opening round of the British Rally Championship, the National Breakdown Rally, held as usual in the fabulous Yorkshire forests. It was a very snowy event and he was really showing his talent in the difficult conditions. One thing I had come to recognise, over years of co-driving for many different drivers, is the point at which they start trying too hard and which usually leads to an accident! I felt Andrew was getting carried away in the snow. We were experiencing quite a few close calls, so I suggested he backed off his pace a touch as my own self-preservation instinct kicked in! Andrew was having none of it, insisting he was in total control, though I could see he wasn't! Things became a little tense and eventually I told him in no uncertain terms that he was driving 'over the top' and that we would shortly be heading for an accident if he carried on at the same pace. I also pointed out that it would not go down well with his new employers if he seriously damaged the car on his first rally for Vauxhall. He seemed unhappy that I was telling him how to drive, but that was exactly what I had been employed to do.

On one particularly snowy forest stage I was forced to give him another warning to slow a little in the appalling conditions but he continued to ignore me. It was only a matter of time and, sure enough, we went off the road into a deep snow drift. It had been inevitable, and we were stuck there for over twenty minutes before the enthusiastic spectators dragged us back onto the road. However, our rally was more or less over from the perspective of a decent result. Andrew was distraught and I think he learned something that day. He was a hugely talented driver for his tender years and it was important that he retained his confidence, so no-one in the team made a big deal about the 'off'.

We were looking forward to the Circuit of Ireland Rally. The Astra was a great tarmac car and, as expected, we steamed away from the rest of the Group A opposition in the early stages of the event. Everything was nicely under control and Andrew was driving well, until we overshot a tee junction at night, went through a gate and into a field. There was little grip on the damp grass and I got out to push the car, when a dozen or so spectators ran down to help. However, the stage was very close to the border town of Newry, well-known for being sympathetic to 'the cause'. They took one look at our British registration number and walked away again! I eventually persuaded them to help, and we regained the road, having lost just a couple of minutes.

At the following service area, our team manager, Melvyn Hodgson, came up to me and said: "Andrew tells me you were late calling the note, which is why you went off."

"Melvyn," I retorted angrily, "that is absolute rubbish!"

"I thought so," he said smiling, and walked off.

We continued with no other major problems, though I had a word with Andrew concerning his comment about my supposedly late pace note call. I was pretty angry about it – if it had been my fault, I would have put my hand up.

Unfortunately, four stages from the end of the rally we hit another 'suspicious' patch of Irish gravel, ran wide onto a bank and rolled into a field. The car was a mess but still driveable and the spectators, no doubt the same ones that had caused our accident, enthusiastically pushed us back onto the road. Andrew was nervous as we arrived at the next service area. Melvyn was a large, and occasionally fierce, Londoner who took no prisoners!

"Will Melvyn will be here?" asked my nervous driver.

"Very probably!" I replied.

Sure enough, the considerable frame of our team manager was soon striding towards us, the very sight of his approach worrying Andrew. We braced ourselves for a tirade of abuse but he walked straight by! Andrew couldn't believe his luck. However, all hope was dashed ten seconds later when he passed us again going the other way. He was obviously trying to calm down before turning round for a final approach! He banged on the window, and I opened it cautiously: "I don't f**kin' know what happened, and I don't f**kin' want to know what happened," he bellowed, "but f**kin' cool it, I want you to finish!"

We had a good margin over the next competitor in Group A so we dawdled through the final few stages and took the Class win, to the team's delight, albeit with a battered car.

We rounded off a successful year in the Astra with a Group A win and twelfth overall on the RAC Rally. It seemed a new rally star had been born.

The following year Andrew and I were out again, tackling the Open Championship using the same Astra GTE. In addition, we were to supplement this campaign with an assault on the prestigious National Rally Championship, using one of the fabulous Manta 400s. I was delighted to be re-associated with the car in which I had won the Open Championship a couple of years earlier with Jimmy McRae.

We were to endure a year-long battle with Alistair Sutherland's Metro 6R4, taking turns to win rallies and lead the championship. The 1986 Championship included a visit to the Isle of Man for the Manx National Rally. This one-day, all-tarmac event, would suit our Manta 400 perfectly and, from the start, Andrew powered the car into the lead. We stayed at the head of the field all day but, with a couple of stages to go, we were only leading by a few seconds. On the narrow Curraghs stage near Ramsey we came round a corner to find the road blocked - an Escort had clipped the bank and rolled. Our nearest rival for the win was running a few cars further back which meant that the moment we slowed, and if the stage was cleared quickly, force majeure rules would see us surrender the lead.

I had to think fast. The only way to save our day was to ensure that the stage was cancelled. I needed to find a way of invoking the rule that allocated every competitor, running behind such an incident, with the slowest time of any competitor running ahead of it, who had completed the stage normally. I had to slow attempts to remove the Escort and I needed to despatch my driver from the immediate scene! If the stage was cleared, I didn't want him to be close by to continue the stage!

"Andrew," I shouted loudly, for everyone to hear, "this is a very dangerous situation, run back to the last corner and slow the next cars."

Two or three spectators were struggling to right the up-side down Escort, so I tried to 'help'. As they were pushing the car, I hung on to its side, lifting my feet off the floor and holding it down, but grunting at the same time to appear as if I was pushing! They had my weight to contend with as well. It worked and, in spite of the spectators' best efforts, they failed to right the car!

By now, several other competing cars had queued up behind us. The stage-commander arrived, going ballistic. He organised the rescue effort and soon the stage was cleared. Then there was a stand-off! I told him there was no way we should restart the stage with a dozen or so cars in line-astern. With faster cars mixed in with slower cars, it would create a very dangerous all-out race situation. He wasn't listening though, and threatened to have us excluded if we refused to move.

"OK," I said, "but if anyone gets hurt, it's your responsibility."

That made him think and in the end he relented. The stage was cancelled, and Andrew and I won the rally. The Motoring News rally report did question our tactics though!

Andrew had matured into a fine rally driver, being exceptionally competitive in the Manta, and we enjoyed considerable success on the national scene. As the last round of the series, the Audi National Rally, drew near we were lying second in the Championship behind Alistair Sutherland's Metro 6R4, with a good chance of taking the title.

During 1986, Opel Motorsport in Germany had been developing a new rally car, the Astra 4S, with which they hoped to tackle the World Rally Championship. Melvyn Hodgson had persuaded Opel to loan us their development car for this last event, hoping to give us an advantage over Sutherland's 6R4 and enabling us to take the Championship. The Astra 4S was an amazing car for its day. It had an 'intelligent', computer controlled, four-wheel drive system, ensuring the power was delivered to the wheels offering most traction. The engine was a fire-breathing 2.4 litre unit taken from the Manta 400 but supercharged to well over 350bhp. The torque was simply incredible and we found that we could easily take even the tightest of hairpins in third gear! According to the spectators that we spoke to during the event, the sound of the supercharger whining in the forests, accompanied by the flames shooting out of the exhaust on the over-run, was something to behold.

We had recently tackled a few of the stages being used during a previous rally in the Manta 400. One duplicated stage was in Dyfnant Forest, and happened to be the first stage of the Audi

National event. It was the first forest stage we'd ever attempted in the 4S. It started with a long straight leading to a tight right-hand bend. We remembered that, in the Manta, we had just managed to select fifth gear by the end of the straight, before hitting the brakes to slow for the corner. We were also aware that, on this occasion, several Vauxhall Directors were spectating on the same corner, so we were keen to put on a good show.

We set off down the stage in the 4S and were completely caught out by its speed! Halfway down the straight we were already on the rev limiter in fifth gear and arrived at the corner way too fast! It was a very big sideways moment and we kept our fingers crossed that the computer would sort out the four-wheel drive and help us to recover before the impending accident. Andrew worked manically to reduce our excess speed and we just managed to get round the corner in one piece. We carried on for a few hundred yards before slowing down and breathing sighs of relief. It would have been a complete nightmare had we crashed this unique car in front of an audience of important people! The hierarchy were, however, mightily impressed by the action. Evidently, from the outside, it looked amazing and as if we were actually in control of the car!

However, the Astra was to be rather problematic during the event. The alternator failed and the battery kept losing charge, which in turn interfered with the car's electronics, causing the engine to misfire. There was no spare alternator available but the team managed to source enough batteries for us to finish the event in third place behind the Ford RS200s of Mark Lovell and Stig Blomqvist. Unfortunately, third overall was not good enough for us to win the National Championship and we had to settle for second place behind Sutherland's Metro 6R4.

By the end of 1986, I had decided that I no longer wanted to continue with the same level of commitment and finally retired from the sport.....or so I thought.

CHANGES AFOOT

Things were about to change for me within Vauxhall Motors. The Board had come to realise the value of motorsport to the Vauxhall brand and were looking to expand their activities in this area. I suppose my co-driving role within the GM Dealer Sport team had made me a prime candidate to spearhead the search for additional activities, so I was called in for a meeting with Peter Batchelor, the Director of Marketing. He explained that they were keen for me to move from the Fleet Sales Division to take up a new position within the Marketing Group.

The role they had in mind was for me to take over responsibility for motorsport internally and also head up Vauxhall's Product Promotion section. I readily accepted the promotion – this was a step up the ladder and I would officially be an 'Executive', which brought additional benefits by way of an increased salary and a permanent, rather than a job related, company car! It also meant that I was to continue my long standing association with the members of the GM Dealer Sport Committee, working with them in support of Vauxhall's motorsport activities.

During the late 1980s GMDS had been running a successful programme of circuit activities in tandem with the rally programme. John Cleland was racing an Astra in the British Saloon Car Championship, following on from his well-known exploits in the Carlton Thundersaloon, the fire-breathing V8 monster that was so popular with race fans.

My search was now on for new motorsport avenues to fulfil Vauxhall's enhanced ambitions. In Germany, Opel had recently created a new single-seater, slicks and wings, one-make racing series, known as Formula Opel Lotus. They had commissioned Adrian Reynard to design and build the car from his Reynard Racing headquarters in Bicester. The car used a modified Astra 16 valve unit as its power base, the superb engine lending itself perfectly to the role. This was too good an opportunity to miss so I set about creating a new championship for the UK and Formula Vauxhall Lotus was born, to be introduced the following year.

Few of us within Vauxhall realised at the time how massively successful this series would be. Along with Opel's European Championship, it was to spawn many of the future Formula One stars. Major teams were attracted to the UK Series and, over the following years, top names including Montoya, Coulthard, Barrichello, and Hakkinen all enhanced their skills and reputation competing in our championship. Other notable names included our first ever champion, Alan McNish, who, following on from his F1 career, went on to be a leading driver in the World Sportscar Championship. We also saw the introduction of a young lady to the championship. Danica Patrick, now a leading-light in the American Indycar Series, started her serious racing career in Formula Vauxhall.

SPEED RECORDS

On the promotional front, I had carte blanche to have some fun over the next few years, so I decided to create a few speed records. We took a Carlton GSi, had it 'chipped' by Swindon Racing Engines for increased performance, and borrowed a caravan from the Swift Group. We took the outfit to the Millbrook Testing Ground's high speed 'bowl', along with some racing and rally drivers, including John Cleland, Dave Metcalfe and Harry Hockly. Our intention was to create a new speed record for a car and caravan combination over a 24 hour period. The outfit was lapping in the outside (fast) lane of the bowl at around 112mph!

We came across a snag though. At these speeds, the caravan was drifting slightly, with its offside tyre wearing too quickly and having to be replaced at regular intervals. We phoned the local ATS Tyres depot and they despatched a fitter with a number of new tyres to replenish our dwindling stock. In the end, we managed to cover the 24 hour period at an average speed of 102mph, which all goes to prove that caravans needn't clog up the roads if driven properly!

Flushed with this success, we took the newly launched 16 valve version of the Astra GTE back to Millbrook for a similar outing. The car was completely standard, and this time we averaged 131.5mph over the 24 hour period. The car was once more in the hands of our race and rally drivers, who had to cope with foggy conditions in the early hours of the morning. The drivers had a competition among themselves to see who could drive closest to the outer barriers. I'm not sure who won, but it was probably John Cleland!

DEREK BELL – RALLY DRIVER!

Early in 1987 our motorsport PR Company came up with a plan: we should consider entering Derek Bell, the three times World Sportscar Champion and five times winner of the Le Mans 24 hour race, on the forthcoming RAC Rally. Derek was, by all accounts, up for it and, following a couple of meetings with him, it was all agreed. It was also agreed that I should return, yet again, to the co-driver's seat to partner him. We planned to compete on three or four national rallies beforehand, to give him experience of a very different motorsport discipline.

It was felt that the 220bhp of the 16 valve Astra was probably a bit too much for him to handle – after all he was only used to 1000bhp in his Le Mans winning Porsche 962! So the 180bhp 8 valve version of the earlier Astra GTE was chosen for the programme. We entered three stage rallies in Wales and North Yorkshire and, like the true professional he is, Derek took to rallying in the forests like a duck to water.

However, we did have a monumental crash in the Coed y Brenin Forest when, mid-stage, we entered a fast right-hand bend that had a deep hole on the inside. Cutting the corner, the Astra hit the hole and rose high up on two wheels. Derek applied a little too much opposite lock as the car was in the air and, as the tyres bit into the forest road again, the Astra turned sharp left, crashing head-on into an unyielding rock face and launching itself into a series of rolls. The car finally stopped on its wheels but, with every panel smashed and the roof crushed, I was trapped in my seat. It was a very big accident and I looked out of the broken windscreen to see Derek's racing driver instincts kick in as he ran down the stage out of harm's way. Suddenly he stopped, realising that, for once, he was not on his own and had a co-driver to rescue! He ran back and dragged me, in a tight head-lock, out of the wreckage damaging my neck in the process. Up to that point I had been uninjured!

November came and by now Derek was quite a seasoned rally driver and really looking forward to the RAC Rally. Sadly, it was to be a rather short, though highly publicised, rally for us. The Weston Park Sunday spectator stage contained a ford that we had noted, during the recce, was only about six inches deep. On the day of the event, however, someone had seen fit to dam it and it was now about two feet deep! We realised that it was much deeper as we approached and slowed to drive carefully through the newly formed lake. The engine stopped dead. Water had been sucked in through the low-sited air intake and into the cylinders causing the engine to 'hydraulic', instantly bending the con-rods. We were pushed out by the ever enthusiastic marshals and attempted to restart the engine. After a few minutes the water in the cylinders drained into the sump, 'unlocked' the pistons and the engine fired into life. It sounded terrible, but we made it to the next service area where the oil and filters were changed.

The whole episode was captured by television cameras, both at the scene and via our on-board camera which was wired for sound. The footage was played out many times over the following days and weeks, with our on-board swear words 'bleeped' out!

We continued, more in hope than anticipation, but on the next stage, Oulton Park, the engine cried enough and our rally was instantly over.

It was a great shame and we were all hugely disappointed. Melvyn Hodgson immediately invited Derek to have another attempt the following year and the deal was agreed on the spot.

LISTEN TO ME!

Derek and I took part in a couple of forest stage rallies during the second half of 1988, settling him back into rally mode. There were no problems and we finished well on both occasions. The air intakes on the Astra had, by now, been relocated to a much higher under-bonnet position!

We arrived at the Harrogate start of the RAC Rally, hoping for better luck than the previous year and feeling fairly confident of a good run. However, on the Sunday morning of the start we woke to find that five inches of snow had fallen overnight. Derek was horrified.

"What happens now, old boy?" he enquired. "Do they cancel it?"

"You still haven't quite got your head around this rallying lark have you, Derek?" I replied, laughing.

The first stage was at Lightwater Valley, a few miles north of Harrogate. This was a combination of farm tracks and roads through a theme park, which were completely covered in deep snow.

"Right," I said at the stage start, "listen Derek, this is one of the 'Mickey Mouse' spectator stages and it is pretty meaningless to the overall rally result. You can't gain much here but you can lose an awful lot if you don't respect it, especially in these conditions."

"OK, understood, old boy," replied Derek.

He hadn't really listened though and got completely carried away in front of the thousands of spectators. One section bordered a field full of cabbages, frozen solid in the minus five degrees temperature of the previous few nights. We went off the road and into the field at a high rate of knots, ploughing sideways through a few hundred cabbages and sending them flying through the air like Howitzer shells. If they had hit any of the spectators there would, undoubtedly, have been casualties! We arrived at the finish and I gave him a bit of a lecture. "Sorry, old boy," he apologised, "but it was bloody good fun wasn't it?"

The poor Astra had taken quite a battering and the bottom half of the nearside bodywork was badly damaged. Melvyn was not happy and took me to one side to gently remind me that it was my responsibility to get Derek, and the car, safely to the end.

Later, we arrived at the first stage of the Kielder Forest complex, the largest man-made forest in Europe and, as we approached, I'd never seen a more beautiful sight. It was dark by now and the snow was literally a foot thick, with the heavily laden trees looking like something on a Christmas card. Even the four-wheel drive cars were having difficulty reaching the stage start and I really didn't think we had a hope in hell of surviving the following forty or so stage miles intact. We were surely destined to spend the rest of the night in a snow drift!

We were running number seventeen on the road and, by the time we attempted the stages, the only thing we could do was try to keep the car within the deep ruts formed by earlier competitors. Had we touched the soft snow on either side, it would have been curtains. Derek was coping remarkably well and we were posting reasonable times, in spite of the conditions, the likes of which I had never seen on a rally before. I was assisting, as usual, by reading the OS maps and one particular section sticks in my mind. I detailed the road ahead to Derek as we powered through the stage:

".....a very long fast open right bend for a good half mile Derek, followed by a similar fast bend to the left over six hundred yards."
After the left-hander I continued:

"Straight now for three hundred yards, over the brow and down to a tee junction where we turn left - watch for the arrows."
We crested the brow.........to find the snow had disappeared and was replaced by a replica of Nottingham Ice Rink! I couldn't work out what was going on but Derek hit the brakes, locked up, and in Torville and Dean style pirouetted a couple of times. The oil light came on to announce that the engine had stalled and we went off backwards at the tee junction!

"OK, lights off." I said, knowing the hot engine needed plenty of electrical 'spark' to restart it quickly. After a short while, it fired up.

"OK, lights on." I said, and, as the auxiliary lights lit up the stage, I couldn't believe my eyes. In the direction from which we had just arrived, half a dozen lads were out with their curling brushes re-polishing the ice! I got the impression they could have even run in front of the car dictating which side we would go off! Evidently, they had been up there for hours, trampling down and then polishing the compacted snow. I was told that it caught out most of the other competitors too. Brilliant!

We somehow survived this first group of long Kielder stages and entered a service area before tackling the final three. John Nixey approached and told me that Michelin had recommended we change to snow tyres for the remaining stages, but I declined. Snow tyres were notoriously puncture-prone and, running seventeenth car through the stages, we were encountering a large number of rocks. I felt our normal forest tyres would be a safer bet.

"Listen, youth," barked Nixey. (Youth? Youth? I was 45 years old!) "You might well be the f**kin' boss out of the car, but right now, I'm the f**kin' boss and you'll take the snow tyres!"

"OK, John," I replied, "but if we lose time through a puncture, I'm blaming you."

We entered the next stage and promptly punctured! I was livid and my mood was not improved when, as I was changing the punctured wheel after the stage, I was very nearly run over by the following car as it overshot the stage finish on the ice!

The rally continued through the next three days, with snow and ice on every single stage. We had many incidents and every night our latest spin or 'off', captured by our on-board camera, was broadcast for some light relief at the end of the BBC News bulletins.

We survived to reach the forests of Yorkshire, where the snow had more or less disappeared and Derek was finally able to stretch the Astra without fear of sliding off the road on ice. He was in his element and, on the penultimate stage in Dalby Forest, had completely switched off from listening to any of my directions. On one particularly fast straight I honestly think he imagined he was back in his Porsche on the Mulsanne Straight at Le Mans!

"OK, Derek," I said, "at the end of this straight, just over the crest that's ahead, there's a firebreak and the road goes ninety left so caution please."

There was no response.

"Slow down Derek!" I stressed. "It's here, ninety left......it's here............HERE!"
Braking hopelessly late, we slid straight on through some tapes and nosed up the firebreak. As he reversed out, I said, somewhat exasperated:

"OH DEREK, WILL YOU LISTEN TO ME...........PLEASE?"

Little did I realise that those words would resonate with so many people. It was, of course, broadcast to the country on the evening's BBC News and appeared several times on Wogan's 'Auntie's Sporting Bloomers' programme! To this day I still have people coming up to me and saying, "Will you listen to me, please!"

A few miles later, on the same Dalby stage, we passed Austin McHale, the very quick Irish driver, with his Sierra Cosworth parked on the side of the stage. He was just closing his door to continue, having cured whatever problem he'd encountered, and set off behind us.

"Keep an eye out for him coming up behind, Derek," I said, "and we'll let him pass."

"OK, old boy, he's coming now."

We moved over just before a sharp right-hand bend, but McHale lost control on some ice at the side of the road and came past us spinning, and went off! We continued on the stage.

"He's coming again!" said Derek, a little later.

"OK mate," I said, "there's a hairpin left just over this crest, pull off on the right-hand side and let him pass."

With just two stages left, I was determined not to let anything prevent us from finishing the rally this year!

We pulled up and I looked over my shoulder. I was horrified to see the Sierra Cosworth careering over the crest, backwards, and heading straight for our stationary car. McHale had lost control again! "Oh, quick......move!" I shouted, "........MOVE!"

It was too late and McHale's Sierra hit the side of our car with a loud 'bang'. Derek shot off like a startled rabbit and we completed the last three miles of the stage with the tyre rubbing on the damaged bodywork and screeching every time we hit a bump. It was all too much for me and I collapsed in laughter, unable to speak until the finish of the stage!

We arrived back at the finish. Derek was elated and I was pleased that I had managed to guide him safely to the end of the rally. We finished twenty-eighth overall and Derek was the fourth highest placed British driver. A pleasing result and I'd had a fantastic time with the World Champion. He is such a gentleman and brilliant fun. I will never forget our time together.

CAUTION, CAUTION, CAUTION!

I was pretty busy by now promoting our motorsport successes from my Luton office and still on the lookout for additional opportunities. John Cleland was going great guns in the British Saloon Car Championship in an Astra GTE, winning his class at every meeting. The series was dominated by the dozen or so 500bhp Sierra Cosworth RSs in the hands of Andy Rouse and other leading touring car drivers. However, the overall driver's championship was not just decided by outright race wins. Class wins attracted just as many points and while his Astra never finished inside the top ten overall, his class domination saw him win the Championship.

As far as I was concerned my co-driving days were over but I was to be proven wrong yet again! There were to be two other opportunities during 1989 for me to dust off my, now ill-fitting, overalls. Opel Sweden entered Mats Jonsson's Kadett GSi on the Welsh International Rally and asked me to co-drive for him. Mats had won the Swedish Championship in the past and I enjoyed his company. Our rally was spoilt by punctures but we nevertheless finished a creditable tenth overall.

Later in the same year I was also to sit beside the ultra-quick German Champion, Joseph 'Sepp' Haider, on the RAC Rally, in an Opel Kadett GSi. It seemed I was not able to shake off the 'pull' of the forests.

Sepp was actually an Austrian and owned a hotel in the ski resort of Saalbach. He had also been a successful downhill skier in earlier years representing the Austrian National Ski Team in the European Series.

During the recce for the Sunday stages we were driving slowly through the Trentham Gardens stage, near Stoke-on-Trent. The stage had been used on previous RAC rallies and I remembered that one fast section, running through a wooded area, contained a bad bump. It was very soft ground and the bump didn't become noticeable until a few cars had passed over it at competitive speeds, when the road on its approach became 'ploughed' into a huge hole. I told Sepp I was going to add a caution to the notes.

"No, no, no!" he said. "There is no problem there, no caution please!"

I tried to explain that it could well be dangerous by the time we approached on the event itself, but he disagreed, so the caution was left out of the notes. As we powered down the straight on the event itself we were flat out, and travelling at some considerable speed. At the last second he spotted the huge hole that had, by now, opened up, but it was too late!

"OH........CAUTION, CAUTION, CAUTION!" he shouted over the intercom just before we hit the bump! There was a huge 'bang' and the car leapt high into the air. As it came down I hit my 'funny bone' on the roll cage and paralysed my arm. It was far from funny but we did have a laugh about it on the following road section. Sadly a broken drive shaft was to finish our rally in the Dovey Forest stage in Wales. We were unable to climb a steep section when the limited slip differential overheated and gave up the unequal struggle of one-wheel drive.

So that was it, supposedly my last ever competitive outing in a rally car. I'd had a fantastic rallying career co-driving for some of the top rally drivers in the world and had enjoyed (nearly!) every minute of it. In many ways it was a sad day, but, on the other hand, I was very busy in my motorsport role at Vauxhall Motors and there was a great deal more to be done in the coming years.

With regard to co-driving, however, I was wrong yet again!

1990 AND BEYOND

During 1990 I received a telephone call from John Kirkpatrick, owner of the famous Jim Russell Racing School based at Donington Park Circuit. He explained that he had commissioned Ralph Firman, of Van Diemen Racing Cars, to design a new chassis to replace the school's ageing fleet of Formula Ford cars. He asked if we had a suitable engine for these new cars and we met to discuss the options a few days later. It quickly became obvious that our 1600cc fuel-injected Nova GTE engine would fit the bill perfectly and a deal was done to supply the units at a very special price!

I was invited to the JRRS Annual Dinner and Awards night later in the year and took along our enthusiastic Director of Marketing, Peter Batchelor, to see the unveiling of the new car. It looked fantastic and Peter took me to one side.

"That would make a really good one-make series to supplement Formula Vauxhall," he said. "Work out a fully costed proposal and come and see me." A few days later we met, my proposal was accepted and Formula Vauxhall Junior was born.

This also turned out to be a very successful series and became synonymous with the ultra-close racing expected from the very young drivers taking part. Dario Franchitti was our first Champion and he went on to become a huge star in the American Indycar Series.

In the meantime, GM Dealer Sport had changed its name to Vauxhall Dealer Sport, reflecting the fact that the Opel badge had been dropped totally from the UK market, and every motorsport activity was, in the future, to be run under the Vauxhall banner.

The British Touring Car Championship was now at the forefront of Vauxhall's motorsport activities. There was still a strong commitment to rallying, however, with the likes of Mark Higgins, David Llewellin and Dave Metcalfe driving the Astra GTE's, these efforts still being largely funded by the dealer levy and administered by the Dealer Sport Committee.

MAKE IT ICE!

I joined David Llewellin on the 1991 Monte Carlo Rally. We weren't competing unfortunately, but making ice-notes for Louise Aitken-Walker's Astra GTE entry. It was great fun and David and I had a ball.....and a few scrapes! We were waiting at the start of one stage, leaving it as late as possible before running through to add ice or snow information to the notes. Several other ice-note crews in front of us set off and we moved forward to follow them only to be prevented from entering the stage by a French Gendarme! He flatly refused to allow us to pass, insisting the road had now been closed. By our calculations it hadn't and we argued as best as we could in schoolboy French that we should follow the other ice-note crews that had just departed. He was adamant, however, that we would not be allowed into the stage. Eventually, an exasperated Llewellin said over the intercom:

"F**k this, we're going!" and he floored the throttle. Three shots were fired as we raced away! We never found out if they were actually aimed at us, or whether they were simply warning shots, and we didn't stop to find out! There were, however, no bullet holes found in the car!

In the middle of another stage, the car 'jiggled' on a slippery patch of road. We stopped and reversed back to look at the surface. "It's OK, just mark it as damp," said David. At that very moment an enthusiastically driven Fiat Punto, full of young spectators, flew past. The driver lost control and slammed into a wall on the outside of the corner. Llewellin saw that they were OK, thought for a second, and then said: "Nah, make it ice!"

After the event we had an excellent night in our Monte Carlo hotel bar. I finally retired to bed at about two in the morning and promptly fell asleep. Shortly afterwards I was woken by a gentle but persistent knock at the door. I got out of bed cursing and opened it. There was a pause, followed by a loud metallic crashing and banging as a load of chairs, ash cans and waste baskets, all piled on top of one another, fell on top of me. I knew exactly who it was.........Llewellin! I could hear him crying with laughter just around the corner in the corridor.

Melvyn Hodgson had retired early that night, not feeling at all well. The following morning, I was having breakfast with him when Llewellin walked into the restaurant.

"Go with me." I whispered to Melvyn.

"What?" he asked.

"Just go with me!" I insisted.

"Mind if I join you?" asked David.

"No, please do." I said and continued my conversation with Melvyn.

"Anyway," I said, "don't worry Melvyn, we'll find out who it was and I'll make sure he never works for the team again."

"What's all this about?" queried the increasingly alarmed driver.

"Oh," I replied, "Melvyn had to go to bed early last night feeling really unwell. He'd just managed to go to sleep when some idiot knocked on his door. When he opened it, a pile of stacked chairs and waste baskets fell on top of him and a chair leg hit him in the eye and has badly damaged it." Melvyn went along with the fun and placed his hand over one eye wincing in pain. Llewellin reddened up and looked really worried.

"I know who that was," he said, trying to wriggle out of the situation. "It was Steve Bagnall!"

Steve was Volkswagen's rally boss and was staying in the same hotel. We never let on to David that we knew the truth!

HEY YOU, BOY!

In 1992 Vauxhall appointed a new Chairman, an American, Bill Ebbert, who came direct from our parent company, General Motors in Detroit. It was always a worrying time when a new Chairman arrived for they usually had pretty strong views on the direction they wanted to take the company and everything was at risk. I was summoned to Bill's office to present our motorsport activities. I had put together a presentation of overhead slides (no 'PowerPoint' in those days!) with a selection of photographs and videos. He showed some interest in the Touring Car activities, acknowledged Formula Vauxhall and Formula Vauxhall Junior but sat bolt-upright when he saw some footage of rallying. I had carefully selected the rally video content and it strongly featured the impressive Dave Metcalfe's Nova in action.

"What the hell is that?" asked Bill, now giving

me his undivided attention, so I explained how stage rallying worked.

"I gotta have a piece of that action!" he drawled. "Can you fix that for me?"

It gave me a great opportunity to get the new man 'on-board' and I set about making plans for his rallying debut. I found a stage rally that was to be held in the classic North Wales forests, phoned the organisers and arranged for Dave and the Nova to act as course opening car with our new Chairman co-driving. The big day came and Bill arrived at the start resplendent in his new overalls and crash helmet! I took Dave to one side and told him to take it steady – I explained that we could not be the cause of our new Chairman's heart attack! "No problem, nice and easy," he promised.

Bill's wife, Mary, had come along and wanted to see some of the action, so we walked a little way in from the end of the first stage in Clocaenog Forest. We stood on a twisty but fast section, just before a 90 left bend and shortly after a crest – from where Mary said she would take some photographs. After ten minutes we heard the approaching Nova and I winced - it was being driven absolutely flat out! The noise of the screaming engine got closer and closer and suddenly the car burst into view. It leapt over the crest at high speed, sideways and in the air! Metcalfe struggled to scrub the speed off for the 90 left, the car snapping from side to side. Mary screamed! Taking to the ditch on the outside of the corner the car roared off, engine still at maximum revs as it flew down the finish straight. It was vintage Metcalfe, but not what was required!

We arrived at the following service area to find our Chairman pacing up and down, furiously puffing on a cigar. He spotted me and shouted for me to go over to him. I approached apprehensively. "Hey you, boy," he snapped, "you got me into this bloody mess, now you get me out of it!" I could already imagine the cuts to my motorsport budget going through his head, so I called Metcalfe and summoned him to my car.

"What the hell are you doing?" I demanded. "I told you to take it easy!"

"I am," he insisted.

"Dave," I replied "we were watching at the end of the last stage......................"

"Oh," he said smiling, "sorry about that!"

Evidently he did slow for the next couple of stages, before an increasingly confident Bill insisted he went at full chat again! Our new Chairman was a convert and our motorsport budget was secure for the next three years of his tenure.

His secretary complained to me afterwards that she couldn't get any work out of him the following week – he was spending all day on the phone telling his Detroit buddies the story!

HE ASSUMED IT WAS FLAT!

I'm not sure how it happened, but I found myself co-driving for Dave a few weeks later and sitting at the start of the first stage, Harwood Dale Forest, on the York National Rally in the diminutive Nova GTE. I had promised myself three years earlier that my co-driving days were over, so how this came about is beyond me!

"Right, Dave," I said, "this stage turns left through a narrow forest gate in two hundred yards and it's then straight for six hundred yards before entering a very fast, gradually tightening right-hander, which finishes in a nasty ninety right – I'll warn you as we approach it."

"OK," replied Dave. We set off, turned through the gate and onto the fast straight. Flat out, we entered the tightening right-hander, with me now telling him to slow for the approaching, and unsighted, 90 right. He took no notice!

"Blimey," I thought, "I know this bloke's quick but this is ridiculous!"

"Slow down Dave!" I shouted. "It's tight ninety right......here!"

There was still no response so I elbowed him urgently and pointed. He hit the brakes way too late and we entertained the dozen or so spectators with a huge moment! Neither of us had realised that our intercom had failed shortly after the start! Afterwards, Dave said he took my silence to assume it was flat!

What a driver he was though - we flew through the forests, arriving at the last stage lying third overall against much more powerful opposition. Unfortunately, we broke a driveshaft just five miles from the end of the stage, with the resultant time loss dropping us to ninth. It was a memorable event and, I assumed, definitely the very last time I would sit in a rally car!

WEATHERCOCK

Vauxhall Dealer Sport entered Dave and the Nova on the classic Ypres Rally in Belgium. Mark Bowie, owner of the Lancashire based Vantage Group of Vauxhall dealers, had recently become Chairman of the VDS Committee and we both agreed to John Nixey's request to carry out 'weathercock' duties on the event. Simply put, our role was to visit areas of the forthcoming stages in advance and report weather conditions by radio to the service area, ensuring the correct tyre choice could be made for the rally car. It was a very hot day and we sat sipping a beer on the veranda of a small bar in the middle of a village through which the next stage was to pass. It would also be a great venue to watch the action. At the appropriate time I called John on the radio and reported clear blue skies, temperature in the mid-seventies and a recommendation for slick tyres.

"Are you sure it's slick tyres?" queried John.

"Absolutely!" I replied, and we returned to our beers to await the action.

A few minutes later there was a huge crash of thunder behind us, accompanied by a bright flash of lightning. We turned around and to our horror saw a massive thunderstorm with an associated wall of rain heading towards us and only a few hundred yards away! Had we taken the trouble to look all around us, before transmitting our 'dry' message, we would have seen its approach. I urgently grabbed the radio and called John, but it was too late, the car had already entered the stage on slick tyres. As a result, and rather embarrassingly for us, the Nova spent nine minutes in a ditch having aquaplaned off the road, which effectively denied Metcalfe a top placing.

Nixey was apoplectic! He raged at us and called us every name in the book. We felt very guilty and tried to explain that it was a very easy mistake to have made but he was in no mood for excuses. After he had calmed down, he told us they could see the black cloud from the service area and noticed all the top runners putting wet tyres on.

"No," he had announced confidently to the team, "my weather chaps tell me it's sunny and dry, we'll stay on slicks."

Oh dear! Even though we were the 'bosses' we were in big trouble and we were never asked to carry out 'weathercock' duties again!

A few weeks later we received devastating news. Dave Metcalfe had lost his life in a road accident on the A6 just north of Kendal. We were numb with shock. It appears that Dave was testing a Swedish owned Calibra Turbo rally car, which was being repaired in his workshop, when there was a collision with another vehicle. It was a huge loss for his family, his many friends and for the motorsport fraternity in general. I was proud to be asked to give the eulogy at his memorial service a few weeks later, where I recounted some of our lighter moments with Dave, including the rally with our Chairman. I had a tough time holding it all together and I did panic just before standing up, wondering if my talk was a little too light-hearted. It turned out that it wasn't and it went down well.

PROMOTIONAL FUN!

Towards the end of 1994 Vauxhall launched the Vectra SRi V6. The main thrust of the launch was a six week drive across the USA. The route ran from Washington to Los Angeles, via Texas, New Mexico and Colorado and was divided into weekly segments, with motoring journalists flown out to drive each segment. I was involved with the New Orleans to Santa Fe section and we took along various motoring 'scribes'. It was a fantastic adventure, seeing parts of the USA that were way off the normal tourist trail. We also stayed in some unusual hotels. In Texas we stayed in an Indian encampment with wigwams for rooms and another night was spent on a 'Dude Ranch' where we slept in converted stables. Here we rode horses and followed resident cowboys to round up cattle and in the evening we attended a Rodeo and barbeque.

Many of us had difficulty walking the next morning, not being used to riding horses!

I was not very happy staying in one particular hotel near Houston. The bedrooms were log cabins, built on stilts over an alligator swamp! After we had dinner in the main part of the hotel, we were transported to our rooms by air-boat! It was pitch dark and I couldn't sleep listening to the alligators swishing around under my room, making wheezing sounds. I swore I could even hear them scratching at the door trying to get in! Eventually I got some comfort by switching the bathroom light on! The next morning I was collected for breakfast and told the story of my sleepless night. Every other person sat around the table said they did exactly the same thing, which made me feel a bit less of a coward!

The launch was, as you might expect, a great success!

During February 1995 we laid on a special Vectra SRi V6 treat for the motorsport media. I arranged for John Haugland, the well-known Norwegian rally driver, to put together a fun package at his ice-racing school in central Norway. We chartered a twelve seat Gulfstream 4 executive jet and flew the motorsport journalists from Luton to Dagali airport. I can remember the Spanish Captain 'losing it' during touchdown and sliding sideways down the ice covered runway. He reckoned it was his most exciting landing since leaving the Spanish Air Force!

It was the depths of winter and we had transported half a dozen V6 Vectras to Dagali, where they were fitted with competition studded-tyres. We invited our media friends to blast the cars around the ice-circuit, which was cut into a large frozen lake and was over a mile long – of course we joined them! It was indescribable fun! I had no idea how much grip these longer-studded tyres afforded on sheet ice and we were all drifting the cars at well over 80mph through the faster bends.

Our hotel had a young lady receptionist, just 18 years old. She was invited to have a drive in the Vectras and we were staggered when she blew everyone away! Unbeknown to us, she was the current Norwegian Ladies Rally Champion, a fact that John Haugland hadn't told us beforehand!

Unfortunately, I was the only person to bend a car when I went off into a snow bank and tore the front splitter off!

For the evening's entertainment we had some further treats in store - racing ski-doos. As you might expect, John Cleland and David Llewellin, who both accompanied us on the trip, took the ski-doo racing rather too seriously and I made the mistake of riding on the rear passenger seat of Cleland's machine. He was determined to make me fall off and, of course, he eventually succeeded!

On the second night it was snowing heavily when Haugland turned up with a van full of toboggans. These 'sledges' had three short skis for runners, two at the back and a single one at the front connected to a steering wheel. We all piled into a mini-bus and followed him for several miles up a steep road to a ski resort. Here we were allocated a toboggan for the return run, back down several miles of the same snow covered road. It was pitch dark and snowing heavily. Eventually we managed to gain a little night-vision and set off. It was carnage!

The toboggans had little control and suffered from terminal understeer – everyone was going 'off' in all directions. Llewellin caught a foot in a snow bank and did the 'splits', tearing his groin in the process, spending the rest of the trip in pain, and walking bow-legged! I came round a fast right-hander to find Cleland had fallen off his toboggan and was lying in the middle of the road. Unable to stop, I shouted a warning and he leapt in the air as I flew underneath. Unfortunately, he didn't reach enough height and I was knocked flying! Stuart Harris, an accompanying Vauxhall executive, was the last man down and benefitted from the following Haugland's van headlights. John reported that he saw Harris reach over 50mph on the long final straight! It was huge fun and we all had a ball!

The following day we flew in the Gulfstream to the Jarama Circuit outside Madrid where the journalists were treated to some laps in the BTCC Vectra. It was a fantastic, but expensive, four day trip which nevertheless bought us some excellent coverage in the magazines!

Those were the days when exotic car launches were the norm and which probably hastened General Motors bankruptcy!

TRIPLE EIGHT

Our British Touring Car Championship activities continued with considerable success but it was becoming increasingly difficult for Vauxhall Dealer Sport to fund the rising costs through the dealer levy alone and often Vauxhall had to top up the budget.

In 1995 it was agreed that the Committee would wind up and hand the entire responsibility for their motorsport activities to Vauxhall Motors, transferring all of the costs to Vauxhall's marketing budget. It was the end of an incredibly successful motorsport operation. For many years the Committee and its dealer levy contributions had delivered fantastic success for Vauxhall.

This move transferred the entire motorsport operation to my office, with a significant rise in my budget. Vauxhall's motorsport activities were, by now, considerable and had become an intrinsic part of our marketing activities. In addition to rallying, the BTCC, Formula Vauxhall, and Formula Vauxhall Junior, we had also supported Oliver Gavin's British F3 effort in the Edenbridge Racing Dallara. Powered by a Spiess-tuned version of our 2.0 litre 16 valve engine, Gavin won the Championship in 1995, notching up yet another success for the fantastic power plant that had been used in virtually all of our race and rally cars.

Towards the end of 1996 I received a telephone call from Derek Warwick, the ex-Formula 1 driver, telling me that he and a couple of colleagues were thinking of setting up a new team to compete in the British Touring Car Championship and asked if there was likely to be any opportunity to work with Vauxhall. I assured him that under any other circumstances we would be extremely interested but we were just about to negotiate a three year extension with Ray Mallock, our incumbent BTCC team, but I thanked him for the call. A few days later I arrived at RML's premises, with one of our legal team and a senior chap from our purchasing department, to extend our association. It was not a successful meeting and it became obvious from the outset that we were not going to be able to reach a deal that was acceptable to us. We were unable to agree terms, and we left with no contract in place.

My thoughts quickly turned to who could replace RML. It was quite late in the year and most of the more successful BTCC Teams were already committed in other areas. Remembering the earlier phone call from Derek Warwick, I called him to discuss the possibilities. We arranged to meet the same evening in the Newbury Marriott Hotel and, while sitting in his room, a face peered out of the bathroom. "Is it safe to come in now?" the 'face' enquired.

It was Ian Harrison, ex-manager of the Williams Formula 1 Team during the Senna/Mansell days, who was currently heading up the Williams-Renault BTCC Team! He had been in secret discussions with Derek Warwick and business partner Roland Dane about setting up the new team and didn't want to show his face until agreement seemed possible.

The deal was put together very quickly and contracts were signed within a couple of weeks! The team was to be known as Triple Eight Race Engineering. They already had factory premises in Greatworth Park near Banbury but that was quite literally all they had! There was no furniture, no trucks, no engineers, no mechanics, no design personnel, no manufacturing equipment and no race drivers! The place was, in fact, an empty shell and it was just five months to the first race!

Ian was on the case immediately, sleeping on a camp bed in the new factory and working 24 hours a day setting up the new team. He did a sterling job and we had two shiny new Vectras on the track, ready for the Media Day of the 1997 British Touring Car Championship. Thus started a thirteen year association with this brilliant team, during which Vauxhall dominated the BTCC, taking many race and championship wins with drivers including James Thompson (Piggy's son, whom, you will remember I had known since he was a baby), Yvan Muller, Fabrizio Giovanardi, Jason Plato, Colin Turkington, Matt Neal, John Cleland, Jeff Allam and Derek Warwick himself. To say the least, it had been a bit of a gamble for both parties, but boy did it work out well!

In 1997 we introduced a new saloon car racing championship, the Vectra V6 Challenge. I contracted David Whitehead at Motor Sport Developments (MSD) to develop and build the cars for the one-make series. The modifications were kept fairly simple to keep costs down, but the cars looked, and sounded, fantastic on the race track. Overall, it was a pretty successful championship and produced great racing, but we did suffer from some transmission problems, resulting in regular complaints from team owners and drivers alike! The series was eventually scrapped three years later.

By 1997, the British Rally Championship had become a shadow of its former self. Gone were the ultimate Group B cars, along with their world class drivers. The Motor Sports Association was anxious to try and rebuild the Championship's success of previous years and introduced new technical regulations, which would allow the development of what became known as Kit cars. These cars were restricted to two-wheel drive but there was enough scope for them to be very quick indeed, and they still required a considerable budget to compete successfully. Luckily, at that time, finding budget for an attack on such a high profile series was not too much of a problem, especially as our new Marketing Director, Ian Coomber, was a rally fan. Vauxhall had a long association with rallying and he was keen for us to participate. Volkswagen, Renault and Seat also took up the challenge and some fantastic rally action took place over the next two years.

Ray Mallock was contracted to design, build and develop the car and came up with a fabulous rally example of the Astra.

STEERING IS BROKE!

We spent three days testing at the mid Wales Sweet Lamb Forest stage during the development phase of this new Astra Kit car. Our driver was a young rising Finnish star, Jarmo Kytolehto, and he was anxious for me to sit in with him on the stage and show me how good the car was. I flatly refused, telling him that I would never again sit in one of those bumpy, noisy, and uncomfortable rally cars!

On the third day I was becoming a bit bored and finally succumbed to the team's badgering for me to have a ride in the car. I squeezed into a spare crash helmet and we set off. It was very impressive and I was amazed at the speed of the front-wheel drive car. Its excellent traction out of tight corners and the way it power-oversteered, just like a Manta 400, brought all the old memories flooding back!

Driving very quickly on a fast, but tightening, downhill left-hand bend, with a large drop on the outside, the car suddenly spun, almost rolling, and stopped with two wheels hanging over the drop!

I was surprisingly unperturbed by all this action and quipped: "So Jarmo, it's good to see Finnish drivers can still spin cars."

"No, no, no! Steering is broke.....you can see!" explained the flustered youngster.

The steering had indeed jammed solid and it had been impossible to prevent the car from going off. We were rescued by the service crew and that was the day I vowed that I would definitely never, ever, sit in a rally car again!

We had some success over the next couple of years with the Astra, with Mark Higgins, Neil Wearden and Jarmo driving for us. They were all outstanding drivers and the car was mechanically reliable but, with so much power driving through the front wheels, it suffered from massive tyre wear and subsequent punctures, which hampered their efforts.

ISN'T THIS RATHER STRANGE?

Around this time, I joined the FIA Touring Car Commission to represent Vauxhall Motors. The Commission usually met in the FIA Headquarters in Paris, but occasionally we would travel to other more interesting venues. One such meeting took place in Modena and included a fascinating tour of the Ferrari factory - another was in Monte Carlo the day after the Grand Prix. This particular meeting took place in the Hotel de Paris, where a 'special' rate had been negotiated by the FIA! I remember, though, that the Vauxhall Accounts Department winced when my expenses went in!

We broke for lunch and sat outside enjoying the sunshine. Alec Poole, the Nissan representative, was laid back in his chair.

"Isn't this rather strange?" he mused.

"What?" we asked.

"Well, here we are," he said, "in this playground

of the rich and famous. We arrived by air into Nice and we were brought here by helicopter straight to the Monte Carlo helipad. We are staying in one of the world's most exotic hotels overlooking the famous Casino Square and tucking into this fantastic buffet, complete with a magnificent ice-sculpture on the table."

"So?" we enquired.

"Well," he said, "what have we been talking about all morning? How can we reduce the cost of motorsport?"

We had to laugh at the irony of it all!

I was later to take over responsibility for Vauxhall's sponsorship activities, adding it to my motorsport role. We took the decision to sponsor the RAC Rally via our Network Q Division, replacing the rally's long term association with Lombard. Network Q was a newly formed used-car franchise and it was felt that sponsorship of the event would create a prestigious platform from which to launch the new initiative. We went on to enjoy several years of very successful sponsorship of the rally, with the Network Q brand benefitting hugely from its association with this great event. I also took the opportunity of spreading our sponsorship wings further to include major sailing championships, athletics, junior golf, tennis, the Northern Ireland Football Team and, of course, support of the Vauxhall Rally of Wales which, under Jim Jones' stewardship, became arguably the best event in the Open Rally Championship. Finally, I must not forget the Vauxhall Conference. This football championship was run by some highly motivated people, including some top ex-footballers, and we were treated like royalty at any match we attended!

THE FINAL STAGE

In the years leading up to the millennium General Motors was struggling with very high costs and a falling market. This affected all divisions within Vauxhall, including motorsport. Every year our budgets were reduced, leading to an enforced reduction in activities. As a result, our rally programme, along with the Vectra V6 Challenge, Formula Vauxhall and Formula Vauxhall Junior, all had to be canned. I had an uncomfortable time announcing this to the various teams and drivers, but nothing could be done. We were finally left with just the British Touring Car Championship. The BTCC was, nevertheless, hugely successful for Vauxhall, thanks to the expertise and enthusiasm of Triple Eight Race Engineering. We successfully raced the old style Vectra, the Astra Coupe and the Astra Sport Hatch, before switching back to the later model Vectra. Our success was phenomenal, winning the Drivers, Teams and Manufacturers titles several times.

I took the opportunity of taking early retirement in 2000, but was retained by Vauxhall under contract to oversee the BTCC operation, which I did until 2009.

However, all good things must come to an end. At the conclusion of the 2009 BTCC season and with GM's bankruptcy looming, the decision was taken to pull out of all motorsport activities. This would be the first time for many decades that there would be no works backed Vauxhall taking part in any of the UK's motorsport championships.

I finally left the sport after having a continued association with various motorsport disciplines over the previous 52 years! I was, by now, 66 years old and it had been a long innings.

In 2006 I realised a lifelong ambition by gaining my private pilot's licence, and am now able to spend much more time in the air, though I promise I will never pull any Tony Pond style tricks on my passengers!

I have recently trained to become an MSA Steward, officiating in all disciplines of the sport including karting, hill climbs, circuit racing and, of course, rallying. It's fascinating to see the 'other side' of the sport and, as 'poacher turned gamekeeper', I don't let them get away with much - I've been there, done that, and got the tee-shirt!

I have had a fantastic life in and around the world of motorsport, enjoying every minute of my 52 year involvement. I am not ready to depart this world yet but, when I do, I will leave with no regrets whatsoever.

PICTURE CREDITS

The following photographs were supplied by the copyright holder: www.rallyretro.com

Front cover: *Manta 400 on Scottish Rally*
Back cover: *Profile Mike Nicholson*

Inserts:

Pentti in a jovial mood following our 1978 Mintex win

Pentti in full flow during the 1978 Scottish Rally - we were second to Mikkola

With Jimmy McRae in the wonderful SMT single-cam Chevette

Jimmy McRae jumping for joy on the snowy 1979 Mintex Rally

Me in my 'office' during the 1980 Circuit of Ireland Rally

"It's still oversteering Geoff!" Tony Pond on the 1981 Mintex Rally

Tony Pond pushes the Chevette to the limit on the 1981 Manx Rally

Tony Pond - awesome on the 1981 Manx night section on the way to our victory

Terry Kaby 1983 - what's broken this time?

The Scottish rocks! Terry Kaby in 1983

With Terry Kaby at speed on the 1983 Manx Rally

It's not looking good!
Head gasket failure on 1984 Circuit of Ireland

Kicking up the dust on our way to 2nd overall on the 1984 Scottish Rally - behind Hannu Mikkola again!

We lost an argument with a stone wall - 1984 Circuit of Ireland

Jimmy McRae & Mike Nicholson
1984 British Open Rally Champions

We'll take the round black ones!
1985 Circuit of Ireland Rally with Andrew Wood

Oops! - 1985 Welsh Rally with Andrew Wood

With Andrew Wood in the mighty Astra 4S

The following photographs were supplied by the copyright holder: www.lesashephotography.com

Inserts:

1981 Scottish Rally - happy winners!

Jimmy flies the Manta on the 1984 Ulster Rally

Ready for the night stages on the 1984 Ulster Rally

On our way to 7th overall on the 1984 RAC Rally

1984 RAC Rally in the Yorkshire forests

Nursing a sick engine in Wales on the 1984 RAC Rally

INDEX

Airikkala, Pentti 82-111, 113, 114, 117, 121, 144, 151-153, 166, 168, 181, 186, 187, 194
Alen, Markku 86, 89, 96, 113
Allam, Jeff 283
Anderson, Ian 115
Andrie, Jean-Marc 155, 160
Arthur, Rob 218

Bannister, Steve 57
Batchelor, Peter 238, 260, 261
Bean, Bob 57
Bell, Derek 243-255
Bell, Ricky 170
Birbeck, Chris 57
Blomqvist, Stig 113, 125, 186, 195, 225, 237
Blydenstein, Bill 102, 103, 200
Blydenstein, Frances Mary 102
Bowie, Mark 272

Broad, Mike   14, 146, 185, 188, 193, 195, 196, 200, 201, 217, 220
Brookes, Russell   28, 37, 39, 58, 59, 86, 88, 89, 96, 117, 120, 125, 135, 146, 147, 185, 187, 188, 191, 193-196, 200, 201, 205, 206, 209, 210, 215-223
Brown, John   58
Buckley, Ger   146
Butterfield, John   112, 123

Carpenter, Harry   104
Clark, Roger   62, 86
Cleland, John   239, 241, 242, 256, 278, 279, 283
Coleman, Billy   125, 128, 129, 205, 209
Cooke, Roy   184
Coomber, Ian   284
Culcheth, Brian   71, 74, 75

Dane, Roland   282
Davenport, John   69, 71, 74, 77-79, 82
Demuth, Harold   205
Drummond, Tony   21, 52-56, 67, 76,
Ebbert, Bill   266-269
Eklund, Per   113, 125, 186

Fall, Tony   27
Fisher, Bertie   205, 215, 221

Fowkes, Tony 27

Gallagher, Drew 26
Gallagher, Fred 74, 76, 139
Gerowski, Marek 64-66
Giovanardi, Fabrizio 283
Gormley, Kevin 28
Grewer, Colin (Mad Dan) 21, 42, 78, 111
Grindrod, Ian 138, 157, 169, 189

Haider, Sepp 257, 258
Hannah, 'Hammie' Hamilton 25
Harris, Stuart 279
Harrison, Ian 282, 283
Haugland, John 276-279
Hauksson, Hafsteinn 205
Harryman, Terry 192, 193
Hertz, Arne 202
Higgins, Mark 261, 287
Hinchliffe, Barrie 169
Hodgson, Melvyn 230, 231, 235, 246, 249, 264
Hodgson, Peter (Yuk) 21, 22, 44, 45
Hockly, Harry 241
Horton, John 162

Johnstone, Gerry 82, 83, 133
Jonsson, Mats 257

Kaby, Terry   186, 187, 190, 194, 197, 199
Kankunnen, Juha   217, 218
Kirkpatrick, John   260
Kleint, Jochi   113
Kullang, Anders   125
Kytolehto, Jarmo   286, 287

Llewellin, David   261-265, 278
Lovell, Mark   237

Makinen, Timo   80, 81
Malkin, Colin   27
Mallock, Ray   281, 282, 285
Marshall, Gerry   182, 183
McHale, Austin   205, 253, 254
McRae, Jimmy   84, 86, 88-89, 93, 96, 100, 104, 108, 113-122, 125-140, 144-146, 149, 150, 153-155, 157, 159-161, 163, 164, 168, 169, 171-173, 187-189, 191, 193, 194, 200, 201, 203- 207, 210, 211, 214, 216, 219-221, 223, 232
Metcalfe, Dave   241, 261, 266-268, 270-274
Mikkola, Hannu   86, 88, 89, 99-102, 113, 118, 125, 126, 133, 134, 176-179, 186, 187, 189-191, 193, 201, 202, 204, 205, 209-211, 217, 218, 225, 226
Mouton, Michelle   225

Muir, Ian 84
Muller, Yvan 283

Neal, Matt 283
Nicolas, Jean-Pierre 113
Nixey, John 200, 227, 251, 272-274

Osborne, Mike 17, 18

Pelling, Dennis 21
Plato, Jason 283
Platt, Roger 27-41
Pond, Tony 74-77, 80, 86, 117, 119, 120, 125, 135-138, 141-156, 165, 167, 168, 170-181, 217, 221, 292
Poole, Alec 288, 289
Price, John 62
Price, Mick 13

Ragnotti, Jean 159, 160
Ratcliffe, Stan 9-11
Rohrl, Walter 165, 167, 168, 170-172, 214, 215, 217
Ruiz Jimenez, Antonio 35
Ryan, Pat 59-64, 69, 78-81, 141

Salonen, Timo 113, 119
Sclater, Chris 108

Short, Phil 151, 152
Smith, Peter 57
Sparrow, Will 27
Strathdee, Alex 115, 163
Sutherland, Alastair 232, 234, 235, 237
Syer, Johnson 71, 74

Thompson, Barbara 67
Thompson, David (Piggy) 21, 22, 43-45, 64, 66, 77, 78, 111
Thompson, James 67, 283
Toivonen, Henri 113, 125, 126, 186, 188, 189, 191-193, 196, 205
Turkington, Colin 283

Vatanen, Ari 86, 103, 125, 126, 129, 131-134, 137, 148-150, 178, 186, 187, 192, 193, 196, 211, 225, 226
Virtanen, Risto 104

Waldegard, Bjorn 103, 113, 189
Warwick, Derek 281-283
Wearden, Neil 287
Whitehead, David 283
Wilson, Malcolm 135, 155, 191, 209
Wood, Andrew 227-236